T0347398

CHINA

China in the closing days of its Imperial era are captured in the drawings and paintings of the artist Mortimer Menpes, noted for his portrayals of the Far East, with text by Sir Henry Arthur Blake, who served as Governor of Hong Kong. Blake writes with elegant authority on Chinese life, customs and landscape, including the Temples of the Seven Star Hills, Opium, Life on the Yangtse, Flower Boats, Curious Forms of Gambling and the Houses of the Wealthy, and the pages are enlivened by Menpes' marvellous drawings that bring the narrative to life. Now that interest in traditional China has never been greater, the publication of this classic treasure is indeed timely.

www.keganpaul.com

A SHOEMAKER.

CHINA

MORTIMER MENPES AND
HENRY ARTHUR BLAKE

Routledge
Taylor & Francis Group

LONDON AND NEW YORK

First published 2006 by
Kegan Paul Limited

Published 2013 by Routledge
2 Park Square, Milton Park, Abingdon, Oxon OX14 4RN
711 Third Avenue, New York, NY, 10017, USA

*Routledge is an imprint of the Taylor & Francis Group,
an informa business*

British Library Cataloguing in Publication Data
Menpes, Mortimer
China. – (China Library)
1.China – Social life and customs – 1912-1949 2.China –
Civilization – 1912-1949
I. Title II.Blake, Henry Arthur
951'.04

ISBN 13: 978-0-710-31066-8 (hbk)

CONTENTS

CHAPTER I

CHAPTER II

CHAPTER III

CHAPTER IV

CHAPTER V

CONTENTS

CHAPTER VI

CHAPTER VII

CHAPTER VIII

LIST OF ILLUSTRATIONS

By MORTIMER MENPES, R.I., R.E.

Also 64 Facsimile Reproductions in Black and White

*These Illustrations were Engraved and Printed by the
Menpes Printing Company, Ltd., Watford, under the personal supervision
of Miss Maud Menpes*

CHINA

CHAPTER I

In attempting even a slight sketch of China, its physical features, or some of the manners and customs of the various peoples whom we designate broadly as the Chinese, the writer is confronted with the difficulty of its immensity. The continuous territory in Asia over which China rules or exercises a suzerainty is over 4,200,000 square miles, but China Proper, excluding Manchuria, Mongolia, Tibet, and Turkestan, consists of eighteen provinces, covering an area of 1,530,000 square miles, with a population of about 410,000,000, or about twelve and a half times the area of the United Kingdom, and ten times its population.

This area is bounded on the west by southern spurs from the giant mountain regions of Eastern

1

Tibet, that stretch their long arms in parallel ranges through Burma and Western Yunnan, and whose snow-clad crests send forth the great rivers Salween and Mekong to the south, the Yangtze and Yellow Rivers to the east, to fertilize the most productive regions on the surface of the globe.

It is this conformation that has so far presented an insurmountable barrier to the construction of a railway from Bhamo in Burmese territory to the high plateau of Yunnan, from whence the province of Szechwan, richest of all the eighteen provinces in agricultural and mineral wealth, could be reached. Some day the coal, iron, gold, oil, and salt of Szechwan will be exploited, and future generations may find in the millionaires of Szechwan Chinese speculators as able and far-seeing as the financial magnates who now practically control the destinies of millions in the Western world.

The portion south of the Yangtze is hilly rather than mountainous, and the eastern portion north of that great river is a vast plain of rich soil, through which the Yellow River, which from its periodical inundations is called China's Sorrow, flows for over five hundred miles.

In a country so vast, internal means of communication are of the first importance, and here China enjoys natural facilities unequalled by any area of similar extent. Three great rivers flow eastward and southward—the Hoang-ho, or Yellow River, in the north, the Yangtze in the centre, and the Pearl River, of which the West River is the largest branch, in the south. The Yangtze alone with its affluents is calculated to afford no less than 36,000 miles of waterways. The river population of China comprises many millions, whose varied occupations present some of the most interesting aspects of Chinese life.

The population of China is composed of different tribes or clans, whose records date back to the dynasty of Fuh-hi, 2800 B.C. Sometimes divided in separate kingdoms, sometimes united by waves of conquest, the northern portion was welded into one empire by the conqueror, Ghengis Khan, in A.D. 1234, and seventy years later the southern portion was added by his son, Kublai Khan, who overthrew the Sung dynasty. It was during his reign that China was visited by Marco Polo, from the records of whose travels we find that even at that time the financial system of the Far East was so far advanced that paper money was used by the Chinese, while in the city of Cambaluc—the Peking of to-day—Christian, Saracen, and Chinese astrologers consulted an astrolabe to forecast the nature of the weather, thus anticipating the meteorological bureaux of to-day.

There are, however, still districts in the southern

portion of China where the aboriginal inhabitants have never accepted the position
of complete incorporation with the Chinese
neighbours. In the mountain district between
the provinces of Kwangtung and Hunan a
tribe exists known as the Yu people, in whose
territory no Chinese officials are permitted to
reside, nor do they allow strangers to enter their
towns, which are built on crags difficult of access
and capable of offering a stubborn resistance to
attack. Their chief occupation is forestry, the timber
being cut during the winter and floated down the
mountain streams when in flood. Their customs
are peculiar. Among them is the vendetta, which
is practised by the Yu's alone of all the people in the
Far East. But no woman is ever injured; and even
during the fiercest fighting the women can continue
their work in the fields with safety. Their original
home was in Yunnan and the western part of
Kwangsi, from whence they were driven out by the
Chinese in the time of the Sung dynasty. The Yu,
Lolos, Miao-tse, Sy-fans, etc. (all Chinese names
expressive of contempt, like our " barbarians "), are
stated by Ma-tonan-lin and other Chinese historians
to have been found inhabiting the country when, six
thousand years ago, it was occupied by the ancestors
of the Chinese, who came from the north-west. The
savage inhabitants were gradually driven into the

hills, where their descendants are still found. Their traditions point to their having been cannibals. Intermarriage with the Chinese is very rare, the Chinese regarding such a union as a *mésalliance*, and the aboriginal peoples as a cowardly desertion to the enemy. The embroideries worked by the women are different from those of the Chinese and, I am informed, more resemble the embroideries now worked at Bethlehem. They are worked on dark cloth in red, or sometimes red and yellow.

After the time of Kublai Khan, succeeding centuries found the various divisions of the Chinese again disunited, in accordance with a very old Chinese proverb frequently heard at the present day, "Long united we divide: long divided we unite"; but the final welding took place under Shun-chi, who established the Tsing dynasty in 1644, and imposed upon all Chinese people, as a permanent and evident mark of subjection, the shaving of the front portion of the head and braiding of the back hair into a queue after the Tartar fashion—an order at first resented bitterly, but afterwards acquiesced in as an old custom. To this day the removal of the queue and allowing the hair to grow on the front portion of the head is regarded as a casting off of allegiance to the dynasty. In the Taiping rebellion that raged in the southern provinces from 1850 to 1867, and which down to its suppression by Gordon and Li Hung Chang is computed to have cost the lives of twenty-two and a half millions of people, the removal of the queue and allowing the hair to grow freely was the symbol adopted by the rebels.

To secure the empire against future risings, the Manchu conquerors placed Tartar garrisons in every great city, where separate quarters were allotted to them, and for two hundred and sixty years these so-called Tartar soldiers and their families have been supported with doles of rice. They were not allowed to trade, nor to intermarry with the Chinese. The consequence was inevitable. They have become an idle population in whom the qualities of the old virile Manchus have deteriorated, and supply a large proportion of the elements of disorder and violence. Of late, the prohibition against entering into business and intermarrying with the Chinese has been removed, and they will ultimately be absorbed into the general population.

From the point of view of a trained soldier these Tartar "troops" were no more than armed rabble, with the most primitive ideas of military movements; but in the north the exigencies of the situation have compelled the adoption of Western drill, adding immensely to the efficiency but sadly diminishing the picturesqueness of the armies—for there is no homogeneous territorial army, each province

A QUIET CANAL

supplying its own independent force, the goodness or badness of which depends upon the energy and ability of the viceroy.

The pay of a Chinese soldier is ostensibly about six dollars a month, which would be quite sufficient for his support were it not reduced to about half that amount by the squeezes of the officers and non-commissioned officers through whose hands it passes. He receives also one hundred pounds of rice, which is not always palatable, the weight being made up by an admixture of sand and mud to replace the "squeeze" by the various hands through which the rice tribute has passed.

While under arms he is clothed in a short Chinese jacket of scarlet, blue, or black, on the front and back of which are the name and symbol of his regiment. The sleeves are wide and the arms have free play. The shape of the hat varies in every corps, the small round Chinese hat being sometimes worn, or a peakless cap, while some regiments wear immense straw hats, which hang on the back except when the sun is unduly hot. The trousers are dark blue of the usual Chinese pattern, tied round the ankles. The costume is not unsoldierlike, and when in mass the effect is strikingly picturesque; but it must not be inferred that all the men on a large parade are drilled soldiers. An order to the officer commanding to parade his corps for inspection not seldom interferes seriously with the labour force of the day. He draws the daily pay of, say, two thousand men, but his average muster may not exceed three hundred. This is a kind of gambling with Fortune at which China is disposed to wink as being merely a somewhat undue extension of the principle of squeeze that is the warp and woof of every Chinese employee, public or private. But he must not be found out; therefore seventeen hundred coolies are collected by hook or by crook, and duly attired in uniform, possibly being shown how to handle their rifles at the salute. The muster over, the coolies return to their work, and the arms and uniform are replaced in store until the next occasion.

The officers are chosen from the better classes, except when a more than usually ferocious robber is captured, when sometimes his supposed bravery is utilized by giving him an army command. The young officers undergo some kind of elementary training. In Canton it was until lately the custom to have an annual examination of their proficiency in riding and archery. In a field outside the city a curved trench about five feet wide and two feet deep was cut for about two hundred and fifty yards. At intervals of fifty yards were erected close to the trench three pillars of soft material each six feet high by two feet in diameter. Into each of these pillars the candidate, who was mounted on a small pony and seated in a saddle to fall out of which would require an active effort, was required to shoot an arrow as he passed at a gallop. With bow ready strung and two spare arrows in his girdle, he was started to gallop along the trench that was palpably dug to prevent the ponies from swerving, as the reins were flung upon his neck. As the candidate passed within two or three feet of the pillar targets the feat would not appear to have been difficult. If all three arrows were successfully planted the candidate was at the end of the course received with applause, and his name favourably noted by the mandarins, who sat in state in an open pavilion close by. But this description would not at present apply to the northern provinces, where some of the armies are apparently as well drilled, armed, and turned out as European troops. That Chinese troops are not wanting in bravery has been proved; and if properly led a Chinese drilled army of to-day might prove as formidable as were the hosts of Ghengis Khan, when in the thirteenth century they swept over Western Asia and into Europe as far as Budapest.

It has been stated that the empire has been welded together by its conquerors, but perhaps it would be more correct to say that it coheres by the almost universal acceptance of the ethics of

Confucius, whose wise precepts—delivered five hundred years before the birth of Christ—inculcated all the cardinal virtues, and included love and respect for parents ; respect for the Prince ; respect for and obedience to superiors ; respect for age, and courteous manners towards all. He held that at their birth all men were by nature radically good, but " as gems unwrought serve no useful end, so men untaught will never know what right conduct is."

The bedrock upon which the stability of China has rested for over two thousand years is the family life, the patriarchal system reaching upwards in ever-widening circles, from the hut of the peasant to the palace of the Sovereign. The house is ruled by the parents, the village by the elders, after which the officials step in, and the districts are governed by mandarins, whose rank of magistrate, prefect, taotai, governor, or viceroy indicate the importance of the areas over which they rule, each acting on principles settled by ancient custom, but with wide latitude in the carrying out of details. Nothing is more charming in respectable Chinese families than the reverential respect of children for their parents, and this respect is responded to by great affection for the children. It is a very pretty sight to see a young child enter the room and gravely perform the kotow to his father and mother. No young man would dare to eat or drink in the presence of his father or mother until invited to do so. Among the princely families the etiquette is so rigid that if a son is addressed by his father while at table he must stand up before answering.

It is sometimes assumed that the custom of wealthy Chinese having two, three, or more " wives " must lead to much confusion in questions of inheritance, but there is no real difficulty in the matter, for although the custom allows the legalized connection with a plurality of wives, there is really but one legal wife acknowledged as being the head of the house. She is called the kit-fat, or first wife, and though she may be childless all the children born of the other " wives " are considered as being hers, and to her alone do the children pay the reverence due to a parent, their own mothers being considered as being in the position of aunts. Strange though it may appear to Western ideas, this position seems to be accepted by the associated wives with equanimity. The custom probably originated in the acknowledged necessity to have a son or sons to carry on the worship at the family ancestral hall, where the tablets of deceased members are preserved. Sometimes instead of taking to himself a plurality of wives a man adopts a son, who is thenceforth in the position of eldest son, and cannot be displaced, even though a wife should afterwards bear a son. A daughter

11

is on a different plane. She is not supposed to be capable of carrying out the family worship, and cannot perpetuate the family name. A daughter, too, means a dower in days to come, so sometimes a father determines, if he has already a daughter, that no more shall be permitted to live. This determination is always taken before the birth of the infant daughter, the child in that case being immersed in a bucket of water at the instant of its birth, so that from the Chinese point of view it has never existed ; but female children who have practically begun a separate existence are never destroyed. In such cases the father is quite as fond of the daughter as of the sons, and in families where tutors are engaged the girls pursue their studies with their brothers.

The power of the parents is practically unlimited, extending even to life or death. A mother might kill her son without fear of legal punishment, but if, in defending himself, he killed his parent, he would be put to death by the lin-chi—or death by a thousand cuts—a horrible punishment reserved for traitors, parricides, or husband murderers. Indeed, while theoretically the woman is in China considered inferior, the kit-fat, or principal wife, is really the controller of the family, including the wives of her sons. She rules the household with a rod of iron,

12

and has considerable, if not a paramount, influence in the conduct of the family affairs. The wife of an official is entitled to wear the ornaments and insignia of her husband's rank, and in the Imperial Palace the Dowager-Empress of the day is probably the most important personage in the empire after the Emperor.

In a Hong Kong paper a short time ago there appeared a paragraph reciting that a wealthy young Chinese, whose mother controlled a large business in Canton, had been spending the money of the firm too lavishly, the attraction of motor-cars and other vehicles of extravagance being too powerful for him. After various endeavours to control him, the mother at length prepared chains and fetters, and had him locked up. He, however, escaped, and the irate mother announced her intention to exercise her maternal rights on his return by cutting the tendons of his ankles and thus crippling him. The account proceeded to say that this treatment is often resorted to by irate parents with prodigal sons.

The most incomprehensible custom among Chinese women of family is that of foot-binding, which is generally begun at the age of three or four, the process being very slow. Gradually the toes, other than the great toe, are forced back under the sole, so that when the operation is complete the girl is only able to hobble about on the great toes. When a

Chinese lady goes out, not using her sedan chair, she is either carried by a female slave pick-a-back, or walks supported on either side by two female attendants. Nevertheless, Chinese women of the humbler classes are sometimes to be seen working in the fields with bound feet. Why their mothers should have inflicted the torture upon them, or why, when they had come to years of discretion, they did not attempt to gradually unbind their feet, seems incomprehensible. The explanation is that not alone would the unbinding inflict as much torture, but slaves and their descendants are not permitted to bind the feet; the deformity is therefore a badge of a free and reputable family, and a girl with bound feet has a better prospect of being well married than her more comfortable and capable sister, upon whom no burden of artificial deformity has been placed. The origin of the custom is lost in the mists of antiquity. One would imagine that the example of the Imperial family ought to have had an effect in changing it, for the Manchu ladies do not bind their feet; but though several edicts have been issued forbidding it, the custom still continues. To Western eyes, bound feet are as great a deformity as is the tight-lacing of European ladies to the Chinese; but physically the former is much less injurious than the latter, which not alone deforms the skeleton, but displaces almost every one of the internal organs.

14

CHAPTER II

THE marriages are arranged in a
somewhat similar manner to that
of the Irish peasants. The negotia-
tions are usually begun by a go-
between instructed by the young
man's family, the etiquette of the
entire proceeding being rigidly adhered
to. There is one insurmountable objection to unrestricted choice—the
bridegroom and bride must not bear the same
name, except in the province of Honan, where the
prohibition is disregarded. The extent of this restriction will be realized when we remember that among
the four hundred millions of Chinese there are not
much over a hundred family names. There may be
four millions of Wongs, but no man of that name
may marry any one of the four millions. As marriage
is the principal event of a Chinese woman's life, she
has crowded into it as much gorgeous ceremonial as
the circumstances of her parents will allow. The day

15

before she leaves her ancestral home her trousseau and presents are forwarded to her new home. At the wedding of a daughter of a wealthy gentleman in Canton a few years ago, seven hundred coolies were engaged in transporting in procession all these belongings, some of the presents being of great beauty and value. The next day the bridegroom arrived with his procession of two hundred men—some on horseback, some armed and in military array—trays of sweetmeats, and numbers of children representing good fairies. The inevitable red lanterns, with a band, led the procession, which was brought up by a dragon thirty feet long, the legs being supplied by boys, who carried their portion on sticks, and jumping up and down gave life and motion to the monster.

The bridal chair in which the bride was carried was elaborately carved and decorated. Its colour was red, picked out with blue feathers of the kingfisher carefully gummed on, which has the effect of enamel. On arrival at her new home, the bride was met with the usual ceremonies, and was carried over the threshold on which was a fire lighted in a pan, lest she should by any chance be accompanied by evil influences.

This carrying of the bride over the threshold is sometimes practised in the Highlands of Scotland, the ceremony having been observed when Her Royal

A STUDENT

Highness Princess Louise, Duchess of Argyll, first entered Inveraray Castle as a bride.

The day after the wedding it is the custom for the bride to cook her husband's rice, the fire being made from wood, which forms part of her trousseau, as she is supposed to bring everything necessary for the purpose to her new home. At a wedding at Macao not long ago, on proceeding to perform the usual ceremony, it was found to the consternation of the bride that no firewood had been sent. Her mother-in-law good-naturedly offered to give her the wood, but this the proud bride would by no means permit. Calling her amah, she directed her to fetch two rolls of silk, each worth about forty dollars, and with them she cooked the rice. When next her father came to see her she told him of the occurrence. He said, " You did right, my daughter ; you have saved your father's face " ; and on his return he promptly dispatched a hundred coolies laden with firewood, which was more than the bridegroom's house could hold.

The ceremony of the " teasing of the bride " is sometimes trying for her, but in good families propriety is rarely outraged. Here is an account of such a ceremony which took place in the house of one of our friends the day after her marriage. The ladies' dinner was over when we arrived ; the gentlemen had not yet come up from their dinner at the restaurant. This evening the bride had gone round the tables pouring out samshu, a ceremony that her mother-in-law had performed on the previous evening. The bride came into the room wearing a gorgeous and elaborate costume of red, the long ribbon-like arrangements over her skirt, huge open-work collar of red and gold, and the bridal crown on her head. The veil of pearls was looped back from her face, and she looked arch and smiling. It was quite a relief to see her after the shrinking, downcast girl of the previous evening. When the gentlemen came the "teasing" of the bride began. She was given various puzzles to solve, two or three of which she undid very deftly. An intricate Japanese puzzle was produced, but the mother-in-law would not allow it to be given to the bride to solve, as she said it was too difficult. The bridegroom came in, and the gentlemen present demanded that he and the bride should walk round the room together, which they did, and were then made to repeat the peregrination. There was a demand that the pearl veil, which had been let down, should be hooked back that all present might see her face. This was done. Then a sort of poetic category was put to her, a gentleman of the family standing near to judge if she answered correctly. The bride was told to ask her husband to take her hand; to ask him what he had gained in marrying her, and so on. The bride had to go round the room saluting and offering tea to the various gentlemen. To one or two relatives she kotowed, and one or two kotowed to her. This, of course, was a question of seniority. Some of the questions and remarks made on the bride must have been trying and unpleasant to any young lady, but being in Chinese they were incomprehensible to us. The idea of the custom is to test the temper, character, and cleverness of the bride.

In the case of people of the lower orders, the ceremony must be more than unpleasant, as there is sometimes rough horseplay, the unfortunate bride being insulted, and now and again pinched severely. But she must show no display of temper or resentment at the rough process, as it would be taken as an indication that she did not possess the qualification of non-resisting submission to her husband.

Each family possesses an ancestral " hall," where are kept the tablets of every defunct member of the family, before which incense sticks are burnt daily, and where once or twice a year all the members of the family within reach attend to lay offerings before the tablets in a spirit of reverence. Should a man disgrace his family he is often repudiated as a member, and at his death no tablet will be placed for him in the ancestral hall. The consequence is that his descendants cannot present themselves for the

19

competitive examinations upon which all official position depends.

The family lands are apportioned annually, and from one particular portion the contribution must be paid towards the expenses of the local temple, including the theatrical performances that cost considerable sums. This portion of the family land is cultivated by each member of the family in turn. If the tenant be a Christian he declines to pay the money for purposes to which he claims to have a conscientious objection. Increased expense therefore falls upon the other members of the family, who feel that the secession has placed an additional burden upon them. The result is a feeling of antagonism to Christianity ; otherwise religious intolerance is not characteristic of the Chinese.

The official hierarchy in China is peculiarly constituted. China is, like all democracies, intensely autocratic, and, within certain bounds, each official is a law unto himself. To become an official is therefore the ambition of every clever boy. At the triennial examinations held in the capitals of provinces, from 150,000 to 200,000 candidates present themselves, who have passed successfully preliminary competitive examinations held annually at various places. To compete in these examinations a certificate must be produced by the candidate that he is a member of a known family. If unsuccessful, he may go on competing at every triennial examination held during his life. Here we see the importance of family tablets in the ancestral hall. No barber, or actor, or member of the boat population may compete.

At Canton, and also at Nanking and other great cities, may be seen the examination halls and the rows of cells in which the candidates—after being rigidly searched to ensure that no scrap of paper or writing is retained that could assist them in the tremendous pending effort of memory—are strictly confined during the time that the examinations last. In Canton there are over eleven thousand; in Nanking there are many more. The lean-to cells are built in rows, and measure three feet eight inches in width by five feet nine inches in length, being six feet high in front and nine feet in the back. From this cell the candidate may not stir, except as an acknowledgment of failure, and many die during the trial. At Nanking during an examination an average of twenty-five deaths occurred daily.

Those who win the prizes are at once appointed to office, and are received at their homes with great honour. Of those who have passed lower down, some are allocated to different provinces, where they remain in waiting at the expense of the viceroy until some situation becomes vacant. Once appointed they are eligible for promotion to the position of

prefect or taotai, or governor, or even viceroy. In all these promotions money plays no inconsiderable part, and a wealthy man may purchase mandarin's rank without the drudgery of examination, as is not unknown in countries that boast of more advanced civilization. In some cases, if a boy shows great intelligence and aptitude for learning, a syndicate is formed by his family, and no expense is spared upon his education. Should he be successful and attain a position of importance, his family rise with him in wealth and influence, and the syndicate turns out a productive speculation. The whole system of examination is one of cramming, which, with competitive examinations, was adopted by England from the Chinese.

The Chinaman who has passed the examination and received what we colloquially term his B.A. degree, even though he obtains no official employment, holds himself above all manual labour, and however poor he may be he belongs thereafter to the body of *literati* known as the gentry, who are consulted on all matters affecting the district in which they reside. It is not easy to know how they live, but the Chinese, like all Easterns, have a great respect for men of letters, and have not yet become so civilized as to abandon higher ideals for the degrading worship of wealth. There is probably found for such men suitable employment in their localities that works into the social economy. There are, of course, among them some lazy ones who, for want of regular work, abandon themselves to the solace of opium-smoking ; but the class is a valuable leaven in the mass of the population.

The viceroy of a province is really semi-independent. His nominal salary in a province of possibly sixty millions of inhabitants is £1000 or £2000 a year, out of which he must supply an army, possibly a navy, internal customs, and civil service.

The taxes are very much at his discretion, with the exception of the settled duty paid by the cultivators on seed corn, that being the way in which the land tax is levied. That paid, the small cultivator is practically free from official interference, and such a man in China if quiet and honest is as free as any man of his position elsewhere.

This method of levying a land tax is most ingenious, and has existed from time immemorial. The land is taxed, not proportionate to its area, but to its productive capacity. Of two plots of equal area one may produce a return from two bushels, while the other being poorer soil will require wider sowing and take but one bushel. All seed must be procured through the official, who levies an equal rate upon it. The same idea governs the computation of distance. A road to the top of a hill may be counted and carriage paid for ten li, the return down hill being measured as five or six, it being assumed that the muscular exertion and time are in both cases being paid for at the same rate.

There are, besides the seed tax, likin, or internal customs, levied on transport of all commodities between districts, and various imposts upon traders. When a man has amassed any wealth he is bled pretty freely. Should a loan be requested it could only be refused at a risk that he would not care to face, and any idea of its repayment is out of the question. But should the demands exceed the bounds of custom there is a check. The people of all classes know pretty well how far the cord may be drawn before it breaks. Should the demands be excessive the people put up their shutters, refusing to do any business, and memorial the Throne. Should such a state of affairs continue for any time even a viceroy would be recalled. Such a state of affairs existed a few years ago in Canton over a proposal to collect a new tax. The people resisted, and at length the viceroy yielded.

The principles on which the viceroy acts are adopted in a lesser degree by all officials, but the people seem to understand the custom and accept it, and in the ordinary business of life justice is on the whole administered satisfactorily.

There are, of course, exceptions. In the province

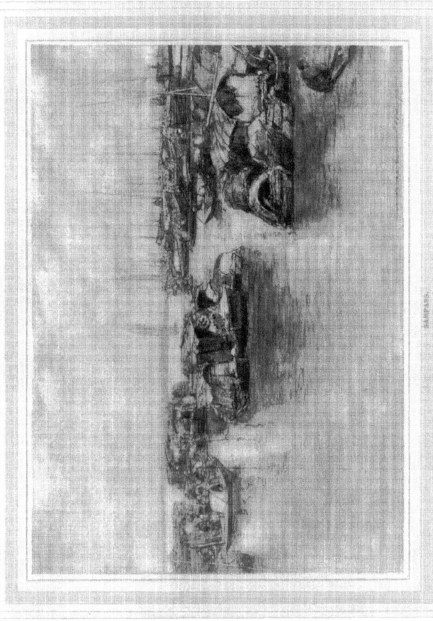

SAMPANS.

of Kwangtung the house of a well-to-do man living in the country was attacked by a numerous band of armed robbers. The owner stoutly defended his house and having killed three of the assailants the robbers decamped. But this was not the end of it, for the indignant robbers lodged a complaint with the magistrate, who summoned the owner of the assailed house to appear, which he did with fear and trembling. He was obliged to pay a hundred and fifty dollars before he was admitted to the presence of the magistrate, who, instead of commending him for his bravery, scolded him roundly, and ordered him to pay the funeral expenses of the three dead robbers. The system of payments to everybody connected with the court, from the judge downwards, would appear to be destructive of every principle of justice; but a highly educated Chinese official, who held the degree of a Scotch university and who had experience of the colony of Hong Kong, when speaking on the subject, declared that he would rather have a case tried in a Chinese court than in a British, for while he knew what he would pay in the first, in the colonial court the lawyers would not let him off while he had a dollar to spend.

When the territory of Kowloon was leased from China and added to the colony of Hong Kong (after some armed resistance by the inhabitants, who had been led to believe that with the change of the flag terrible things would happen to them), local courts were established giving summary jurisdiction to their head-men sitting with a British magistrate, but a proviso was inserted that no lawyer or solicitor should practise in these courts. The result was peaceful settlement of disputes, generally by the arbitration of the British magistrate, at the joint request of both parties to the dispute.

The punishments inflicted in Chinese courts are severe, and sometimes very terrible. The ordinary punishment for minor offences is the cangue and the bastinado. The cangue is a three-inch board about three feet square, with a hole in the centre for the neck. When this is padlocked on the neck of the culprit he is placed outside the door of the court, with his offence written upon the cangue, or is sometimes allowed to walk through the town. In this position he cannot feed himself, as his hands cannot reach his head, nor can he lie down or rest in comfort. Sometimes the hands are fastened to the cangue. The punishment is more severe than that of our old parish stocks, but the idea is the same. Were it in the power of a troublesome fly to irritate a Chinaman, which it is not, he might suffer grave discomfort if the insects were active.

The bastinado is a different matter. This is administered by placing the prisoner on his face, his feet being held by one man and his head

26

by another. The blows are inflicted with a large bamboo or with two small ones. The large bamboo looks more formidable, but though the strokes are heavy they break no bones, and do but little injury. The small bamboos are used in a different manner. Taking one in each hand, the operator sits down and strikes the culprit rapidly with alternate strokes, apparently mere taps. These are hardly felt for the first fifty or sixty taps, and the skin is not broken ; but after this phase the flesh below the skin becomes regularly broken up, and the agony is very great. The recovery from this severe punishment is slow, as the tissues are destroyed for the time being.

These are, however, the light punishments ; torture for the purpose of extracting evidence is still inflicted, and in pursuance of a custom that down to a late period had acquired the force of a law, that no person should be executed except he had confessed his crime, the palpable difficulty of that apparently beneficent rule was surmounted by the administration of torture, until the victim was reduced to such a state of mutilation and despair that he was prepared to state anything that would secure for him relief from his sufferings by a speedy death. It must be acknowledged that the pressure of the torture has now and again secured valuable evidence from unwilling witnesses that may have been capable of independent proof, but as a rule such evidence was utterly untrustworthy.

The following story was told to me by a Chinese gentleman who had personal knowledge of some of the persons concerned.

A son and daughter of two wealthy families were married. At the conclusion of the first evening's ceremonies the bride and bridegroom retired to their apartments, which were separated from the main house. Some time after they had retired, hearing a noise overhead, the bridegroom got up and putting on his red bridal dress he lit a candle and went up to the loft. Here he found a robber, who had entered through a hole in the roof, and who, seeing himself detected, after a short struggle plunged a knife into the bridegroom and killed him. He then assumed the bridegroom's dress, and taking the candle in his hand he boldly went down to the chamber where the bride awaited the return of her husband. As Chinese brides do not see their husbands before marriage, and as she was somewhat agitated, she did not perceive that the robber was not her newly married spouse. He told her that he had found that a robber had entered the house, but had made his escape on his appearance. He then said that as there were robbers the bride had better hand her jewels to him, and he would take them to his father's apartments and place them in the safe. This she did, handing

28

over jewels to the value of several thousand taels. The robber walked out, and he and the jewels disappeared.

Early next morning the father of the bride-groom came to visit his son, and on entering the apartment was told by the bride that she had not seen her husband since he took the jewels to have them deposited in safe keeping. The father on hearing the story went up to the loft, where he found the dead body of his son. He searched about and in one of the courtyards out-side he found a strange shoe.

For the wedding a number of the friends of the family had assembled who were, as usual, accommo-dated in the house. Among them was a young man, a B.A., and most respectably connected. The father taking the strange shoe went round all the guests, who had just arisen. On comparing the shoe he found that it belonged to the young B.A., who was wearing its fellow, the other shoe being that of his murdered son. The father was a cautious man, so instead of taking immediate action he returned to the young widow and questioned her closely. He asked if she could identify the man whom she had mistaken for her husband. She said that she could not. He begged her to think if there was any mark by which identification was possible, and after thinking for a time she answered "Yes," that she now remembered having remarked that he had lost a thumb. The father returned to the guest chamber and asked the B.A. for explanation of his wearing the son's shoe, for which he accounted by the statement that having occasion to go out during the night he had stumbled in crossing one of the courtyards and lost his shoe in the dark, and groping about had found and put on what he thought was his own. Upon examining his hands he was found to be minus a thumb. The father having no further doubt caused him to be forthwith arrested and taken before the prefect. The young man denied all knowledge of the murder, saying that he had a wife and child, was well off, and was a friend of the murdered bridegroom. He was put to the torture and under its pressure he confessed that he was the murderer. The body had been examined and the extent of the wound carefully measured and noted. Asked to say how he had disposed of the knife with which the murder had been committed, and what had become of the jewels, he professed his inability to say, though tortured to the last extremity. He was then beheaded. His uncle, however, and his widow would not believe in his guilt, and they presented to all the superior authorities in turn petitions against the action of the prefect, who ought not to have ordered the execution until corroborative proof of the confession had been secured by the production of the knife and the jewels, but the officials refused to listen to them. At length they appealed to the viceroy, who, seeing their persistence, concluded that there must be something in a belief that braved the gravest punishment by petitioning against a mandarin of prefect rank. He sent for the father and widow of the murdered man, who repeated the story, which seemed almost conclusive evidence of the young man's guilt. He asked the widow if she remembered from which hand the thumb was missing of the robber to whom she had given the jewels. She replied, " Yes, perfectly. It was the right." He then sent for the petitioning widow and asked her from which hand her husband had lost a thumb. She answered, " The left." Then recalling the father of the murdered man he bade him try to recollect if he had ever known any other man wanting a thumb. He said that there was such a man, a servant of his whom two years before he had dismissed for misconduct. Asked if he had noticed the dismissed man during the time of the wedding the answer was that he had, but he had not seen him since.

The viceroy then had inquiry made, and the man was traced to another province, where he was living in affluence, with a good shop, etc. He was arrested, and under torture confessed the crime and told where he had concealed the knife and disposed of the jewels.

31

The knife had a wide blade that coincided with the width of the wound, and a portion of the jewels were recovered, some having been pawned, some sold. The prefect was degraded and punished for culpable want of due care in having executed the man without securing complete proof by the production of the knife and the jewels.

The case is curious as showing the danger that lurks in all cases of circumstantial evidence, and also, from a purely utilitarian point of view, the failure and success of the system of torture. It will always be to me a source of deep gratification that during my administration of the government of Hong Kong, in the case of two murderers surrendered from that colony and convicted after a fair trial and on reliable evidence, I induced the then viceroy to break through the immemorial custom, and have the criminals executed without the previous application of torture, though they refused to confess to the last. The precedent once made, this survival of barbarous times will no longer operate in cases of culprits surrendered from under the folds of the Union Jack, and awakening China may, I hope, in such matters of criminal practice soon find herself in line with the other civilized nations of the world, to the relief of cruel injustice and much human suffering.

CHOPSTICKS

CHAPTER III

In China the gradations of the social fabric as generally accepted are

First.—The *literati* ; for mind is superior to matter.

Second.—The agriculturist; for he produces from the soil.

Third.—The artisan; for he is a creator from the raw material.

Fourth.—The merchant; for he is a distributor.

Fifth.—The soldier; for he is but a destroyer.

However superficially logical this division is, the Chinese have failed to realize that the army is an insurance and protection, wanting which all other classes may be destroyed ; but the fallacy has had an unfortunate influence upon China, for until within a few years the various so-called armies were simply hordes of undisciplined men, whose officers were, as I have before said, sometimes robbers reprieved on account of supposed courage and given command of so-called soldiers. But this is now changed, and such armies as those of Yuan Shi Kai and Chang Chi Tung (viceroy at Hankow) are well disciplined and officered. This viceroy adopted an effective method of combating the contempt with which the army was regarded by the *literati*. He established a naval and agricultural college, and colleges for the teaching of geography, history, and mathematics, and formed all the students into a cadet corps. When I was in Hankow the viceroy invited me to see his army of eight thousand men, who were then on manœuvres in the neighbourhood, and on my arrival I was received by a guard of honour of one hundred of these cadets, whose smart turn-out and soldierly appearance impressed me very favourably. They were well clothed and well armed, as indeed were all the troops, whom I had an opportunity of inspecting during the manœuvres under the guidance of a German captain in the viceroy's service, who was told off to accompany me. I have no doubt that many of those cadets are now officers, and will tend to raise the character of the army.

The importance of agriculture is emphasized by the annual ceremony of ploughing three furrows by the Emperor at the Temple of Agriculture in the presence of all the princes and high officials of Peking. Furrows are afterwards ploughed by the princes and the high officers of the Crown. Agriculture is the business of probably nine-tenths of the population, and in no country in the world is the fertility of the soil preserved more thoroughly. In the portions of China visited by me no idle land was to be seen, but everywhere the country smiled with great fields of grain or rape or vegetables, alternating with pollarded mulberry trees in the silk-producing districts, while extensive tracts of the beautiful pink or white lotuses are grown, the seeds of which as well as the tuberous roots are used for food and the large leaves for wrappers. Nothing in the shape of manure is lost in city, town, or village; everything goes at once back to the fields, and nowhere in China is a river polluted by the wasted wealth of city sewers. On the banks of the canals the cultivators even dredge up the mud and distribute it over their fields by various ingenious devices.

The rural population is arranged in village communities, each village having its own head-man and elders, to whom great respect is shown. Sometimes there is a feud between two villages over disputed boundaries or smaller matters, in which case, if the elders cannot arrange matters, the quarrel may develop into a fight in which many lives are lost. Nobody interferes and the matter is settled *vi et armis*.

But this absence of local government

35

control has its drawbacks; for as sugar attracts ants, so unprotected wealth attracts robbers, and gang robberies are frequent, generally by armed men, who do not hesitate to add murder to robbery. Nor are these attacks confined to distant rural districts. Only a few months ago an attack was made upon a strongly built and fortified country house belonging to one of the wealthiest silk merchants in Canton, who had specially designed and built the house to resist attack, and had armed his retainers with repeating rifles. Twenty-five boats, containing about three hundred men, came up the river, and an attack was made at six p.m. that lasted for seven hours. At length the fortified door was blown in by dynamite and the house taken. Eighty thousand dollars' worth of valuables was carried off, and the owner and his two sons were carried away for ransom. Several of the retainers were killed and thirteen of the robbers.

The country people are very superstitious and dislike extremely any building or work that over-looks the villages, as they say that it has an unlucky effect upon their *fung sui*, a term that means literally wind and water, but may be translated freely as elemental forces. This superstitious feeling some-times creates difficulty with engineers and others laying out railways or other works. The feeling is kept alive by the geomancers, whose mysterious business it is to discover and point out lucky positions for family graves, a body of an important person sometimes remaining unburied for years pending definite advice from the geomancer as to the best position for the grave, which is always made on a hill-side. They also arrange the lucky days for marriages, etc. When the telegraph was being laid between Hong Kong and Canton, the villagers at one point protested loudly against the erection of a pole in a particular position, as they were informed that it would interfere with the *fung sui* of the village. The engineer in charge, who fortunately knew his Chinese, did not attempt to oppose them ; but taking out his binoculars he looked closely at the ground and said, " You are right ; I am glad the geomancer pointed that out. It is not a favourable place." Then again apparently using the glasses, he examined long and carefully various points at which he had no intention of placing the pole. At length he came to a spot about twenty yards away, which suited him as well as the first, when after a lengthened examination he said, with an audible sigh of deep relief, " I am glad to find that this place is all right," and the pole was erected without further objection.

While gang robberies are frequent, there is not much petty theft, as in small towns the people appoint a local policeman, who is employed under a guarantee that if anything is stolen he pays the damage. In small matters this is effective.

CHINA

The necessity for making villages secure against ordinary attack is palpable and many villages in country districts are surrounded by high walls that secure them from such attack. In some, guns of ancient pattern are mounted on the walls.

The prosperity of a town is shown by the number of pawnshops, which are always high towers solidly built and strongly fortified. The Chinese pawnshop differs from those of Western nations, as it is not merely a place for the advance of money upon goods deposited, but also the receptacle for all spare valuables. Few Chinese keep their winter clothing at home during summer, or vice versa. When the season changes the appropriate clothing is released, and that to be put by pawned in its place. This arrangement secures safe keeping, and if any balance remains in hand it is turned over commercially before the recurring season demands its use for the release of the pawned attire. Sometimes very valuable pieces of jewellery or porcelain remain on the hands of the pawnshop keeper, and interesting objects may from time to time be procurable from his store.

Next to agriculture in general importance is the fishing industry, in which many millions of the population are engaged, the river boat population forming a class apart, whose home is exclusively upon their boats. To describe the variety of boats of

38

all kinds found in Chinese waters would require a
volume.   The tens of thousands of junks engaged in
the coasting trade and on the great rivers vary
from five to five hundred tons capacity, while every
town upon ocean river or canal has its house boats,
flower boats, or floating restaurants and music halls,
passenger boats, fishing boats, trading boats, etc.
On these boats the family lives from the cradle to
the grave, and while the mother is working the
infant may be seen sprawling about the boat, to
which it is attached by a strong cord, while a gourd
is tied to its back, so that if it goes overboard
it may be kept afloat until retrieved by the
anchoring cord.   In Hong Kong, where it is
computed that there are about thirty thousand
boat people in the harbour, the infant is
strapped to the mother's back while she sculls
the boat, the child's head—unprotected in the
blazing sun—wagging from side to side until
one wonders that it does not fly off.

The large junks, with their great high sterns
and bold curves, and with the setting sun
glinting on their yellow sails of matting, are
a sight to stir the soul of an artist.   Many
of these carry guns, as the dangers of gang
robberies on shore are equalled by
that of piracy on sea or river, the
West River having the most evil

reputation in this respect. The unwillingness of junks to carry lights at night, lest their position should invite piratical attack, adds to the dangers of collision, and necessitates extreme caution after sunset in navigating the southern coasts of China. These junks convey all the cargo from the coast and riverside towns to the treaty ports, through which all trade between China and foreign nations is exchanged. The high square stern affords accommodation for the crew, but no man dares to desecrate the bow by sitting down there. On one occasion when we went by canal to Hangchow we stopped at Haining to observe the incoming of the great bore that at the vernal equinox sweeps up the river from the bay, and affords one of the most striking sights in the world. While preparing to measure the height of the wave by fixing a marked pole to the bow of a junk lying high and dry alongside, which was most civilly permitted by the junkowner, one of the gentlemen sat down on the bow, upon which the junkowner tore him away in a fury of passion and made violent signs to him to leave the ship. Our interpreter coming up at the moment heard from the irate junkman what had occurred. He pointed out that the bow was sacred to his guardian deity, and such an insult as sitting down on the place where his incense sticks were daily burnt was sure to bring bad luck, if not

ON THE WAY TO MARKET

destruction. Explanations and apologies on the score of ignorance followed, and a coin completed the reconciliation. The origin of touching the cap to the quarter-deck on our ships originated in the same idea, the crucifix being carried at the stern in the brave days of old.

The great wave or bore that I have just mentioned formed about six miles out in the bay, and we heard the roar and saw the advancing wall of water ten minutes before it arrived. The curling wave in front was about ten feet high and swept past at the rate of fourteen miles an hour, but the vast mass of swirling sea that rose behind the advancing wall was a sight more grand than the rapids above Niagara. I measured accurately its velocity and height. In one minute the tide rose nine feet nine inches on the sea wall that runs northward from Haining for a hundred miles. It is seventeen feet high, splendidly built with cut stone, and with the heavy stones on top (four feet by one foot) dovetailed to each other by iron clamps, similar to those I afterwards saw at the end of the great wall of China, where it abuts on the sea at Shan-hai-kwan.

If the land is thoroughly cultivated the same may be said of the waters, for in sea, river, lake, or pond, wherever water rests or flows, there is no device that ingenuity can conceive that is not used for the capture of fish, which enters largely into the food of

6   41

the people; and no cultivation is more intensive than pisciculture, a fishpond being more valuable than ten times its area of cultivated land. Sometimes the pond belongs to a village, and nothing comes amiss that may serve to feed the fish, from the grass round the borders of the pond to the droppings of the silkworms in silk-producing districts. In such cases the village latrine is generally built over the pond; it may, therefore, be understood that Europeans generally eschew the coarse pond fish and prefer fresh or salt sea fish. These pond fish grow very rapidly, and are taken by nets of all shapes and sizes. Sometimes a net forty feet square is suspended from bamboo shears and worked by ropes and pulleys, the net being lowered and after a short time, during which fish may be driven towards it, slowly raised, the fish remaining in the net, the edges of which leave the waters first. In ponds of large area forty or fifty men may be seen, each with a net twelve to fifteen feet square suspended from a bamboo pole, all fishing at the same time. The entire pond is gone over, and as the fish are kept on the move large numbers are thus taken. They are then if near a river placed in well boats and sent alive to market. During the summer months the bays around the coast are covered by thousands of these large square nets. A net sometimes eighty feet square is fastened at each corner to poles, long in proportion to the depth of the water, the other ends of which are anchored by heavy weights. The men who work the nets live in a hut built upon long poles similarly weighted, and securely stayed by cables anchored at the four cardinal points of the compass. From the hut platform the net is manipulated by a bridle rope worked by a windlass. When the net is raised the fish fall into a purse in the centre, from which they are removed by men who row under the now suspended net and allow the fish to drop from the purse into the boat. These nets are set up sometimes in nine to ten fathoms. I have never seen them used in any other bays than those on the coast of China, where, it may be observed incidentally, there is hardly any perceptible growth of seaweed, and one never perceives the smell of the sea or feels the smack of salt upon the lips, as we do on our coasts.

I have said that the devices for the capture of fish are endless, from the large nets just described to the small fish trap set in every trench or gap through which water flows. But they do not end here, for about Ichang, on the Yangtze, otters are trained to drive fish into the nets; and on the lakes and canals a not unusual sight is a boat or raft with eight cormorants, who at the word of command go overboard and dive in pursuit of the fish. Sometimes the bird is recalcitrant, but a few smart strokes on the water close beside it with a long bamboo sends the bird under at once. When a fish is caught and swallowed the cormorant is taken on board and being held over a basket the lower mandible is drawn down, when out pops the fish uninjured, the cormorant being prevented from swallowing its prey by a cord tied round the lower part of the neck.

But the most curious device for the capture of fish is practised on the Pearl and West Rivers, where one sees poor lepers seated in the stern of a long narrow canoe along the side of which is a hinged board painted white. This they turn over the side at an angle during the night, and the fish jumping on to it are dexterously jerked into the boat. In the Norwegian fjords, baskets are sometimes hung or nets fastened under the splashes of whitewash marking the position of rings let into the rocky cliff where the yatches may tie up in an adverse wind. The fish jumping at the white mark, which possibly they mistake for a waterfall, are caught in the net or basket suspended below.

The boat population of the inland waters are liable to the same dangers from armed robbery as are their brothers on land, for the river pirates are a constant source of trouble. Even the large river steamers of the American pattern plying on the West River under the command of European officers are not always safe, though great precautions are taken, as the robbers sometimes embark as passengers if they know of any specie or valuables being on board, and at a given point produce revolvers and hold up the captain and crew, carrying off their booty in a confederate boat. On this account launches are not permitted to tow lighters with passengers alongside lest they should step on board, and in all large steamers the lower deck used by Chinese is separated from the upper by a companion-way with iron railings and locked door, or with an armed sentry standing beside it. About six years ago two stern-wheel passenger boats left Hong Kong for the West River one evening, to enter which the course was usedly laid north of Lintin, an island in the estuary of the Pearl River. The leading boat number one for some reason took a course to the south of Lintin, whereupon the captain of number two came to the conclusion that she was being pirated, so changing his course and blowing his whistle loudly he pressed on with a full head of steam and opened fire upon number one with rifles. Number one returned the fire, assuming that number two had been pirated and was attacking him. He steered back to Hong Kong and made a running fight, a hot fire being maintained until the boats had actually entered the harbour, when they were met by a police launch and the mistake was discovered. Over three hundred shots were fired, but happily nobody was hit. It is not a year since a train of seven or eight house-boats, full of passengers and towed by a steam launch that plies between Hangchow and Suchow on the Grand Canal, was held up by river pirates, who rifled the train as American trains are now and again held up in the Western States of America. These evidences of lawlessness are only the natural consequences of the neglect of the primary duty of a government to make effective police arrangements for the due protection of life and property, for Chinese under proper control are naturally law-abiding and peaceable. The Chinese system does not contemplate any police arrangements outside the principal cities. The small village communities arrange their own police, but there is no official means of combating the more serious offences short of a military expedition. The salutary principle of prevention is ignored and the fitful efforts of government devoted to punishment. This system doubtless acts as a deterrent when the punishment follows the crime so frequently as to impress upon evildoers the sense of its probability. Therefore it is that a strong viceroy makes a quiet province. When pointing out to Li Hung Chang the advisability of controlling a town well known as a headquarters of pirates, his Excellency answered quietly, " We will exterminate them." He ruled the province of the two Kwangs with a rod of iron, and left Canton to the profound regret of every man who had property exposed to attack.

Li Hung Chang was the most able of the many able officials of China. He was supposed to have had strong Russian sympathies, but had he been in Tientsin or Peking instead of Canton when the Boxer trouble was brewing, it is probable that the dangerous conspiracy would never have been allowed to come to a head. The viceroys at Nanking and Hankow maintained peace in their provinces, though the "big knife" movement had its origin in their districts, and Li Hung Chang was as strong a man as either, or stronger. When he left Canton to try to reach Peking it was too late, and the issue had been joined between the Chinese Court and the foreign Powers. He would have done better had he remained in the turbulent southern province that he had ruled so sternly and efficiently. Dangerous as was the Boxer movement, it showed clearly the want of cohesion between the different portions of the Chinese empire. When the trouble broke out in the north, there were a large number of Cantonese students at Tientsin College, whose lives were as unsafe as if they were foreigners. Some Chinese gentlemen waited upon me on the subject. They were in great

47

distress, as they had no means of getting their sons away. They begged me to endeavour to get the young men sent down by the British Consul, and undertook to pay any amount up to ten thousand dollars for the expense of chartering a ship. I telegraphed, guaranteeing the amount, to the British Consul, who kindly chartered a ship for the transit of the young men. The bill of over nine thousand dollars was at once paid by the Chinese gentlemen who had requested my good offices.

The fact is that between different provinces, speaking different patois, there exists in many cases a settled antipathy that has been handed down from the feuds and wars of bygone centuries. To this day the junks from Swatow land their cargoes in Hong Kong at a wharf where Swatow coolies are employed; did they land it at a wharf worked by Cantonese, there would certainly be disorder, and possibly fighting, before the discharge of the cargo.

The traveller in China is impressed with the vastness of its extent, the fertility of its various countries, the grandeur of its rivers, the beauty and boldness of its bridges, the strength of its city walls, the contrast of wealth and squalor in the cities, the untiring industry of the people. A more detailed knowledge compels admiration for their proficiency in arts and crafts.

A GRANDFATHER.

THE WEST RIVER

A journey up the West River leads through the gorges, which gives one an idea of the teeming life of the Chinese water world. The West River is, next to the Yangtze, the one most often coming under the notice of foreigners, for the river is the principal scene of piratical attacks. Indeed, no native boat known to have valuable property on board was, some years ago, safe from attack if it did not pay blackmail, and carry a small flag indicating that it had done so. Perhaps the most curious craft on the river is the stern-wheel boats, worked by man power. Sixteen coolies work the wheel after the manner of a treadmill, four more standing by as a relief. The work is very hard, and coolies engaged in this occupation do not live long; but in China that is a consideration that does not count, either with workman or master. Rafts float slowly down the yellow waters of the broad river—rafts three to four hundred yards long, with the " navigators " comfortably encamped; great junks, with their most picturesque fan-shaped sails ; at every town a crowd of " slipper " boats, as sampans are called, which have a movable hood over the forepart, under which passengers sit. At Sam-shui, the principal station of the Imperial Customs in the river, a dragon-boat shoots out with twelve men. In it are carried a large red umbrella and a green flag, the umbrella being a symbol of honour, while around the sides are painted the honorific titles of the owner or person to whom it is dedicated. From here comes the matting made at Taiking that is sold by retail at ten dollars for a roll of forty yards.

Beyond Kwongli Island the gorges begin, through which the West River debouches on the plains on its journey to the sea. From the island one hundred and fifty acute sugar-loaf summits can be counted, and the tortuous gorges wind past a succession of steep valleys that must have been scored out when the mountain range was upheaved at a period of very great torrential rains.

Above the gorges the old town of Sui-hing is rather featureless, but is a landing-place for the Buddhist monasteries, built at various elevations on the precipitous sides of seven masses of white marble rising from the plain and called the Seven Stars. These old monasteries here and elsewhere are marvellously picturesque, perched as they usually are in situations that can only be reached by steep climbing. The temple is at the base of the cliff, and contains fine bronze figures of Kunyam, the goddess of mercy, with two guardians in bronze at her side. The figures are about ten feet high, and are supposed to be over one thousand years old. There is also a bronze bell said to be of still older date.

Through a great cave and up marble steps the

marble temple is approached in which is a seated figure of the Queen of Heaven. The sculptured figure, like the temple itself, is hewn from the solid rock, the statue of the Queen of Heaven being in a shrine close by an opening through which the light strikes upon the well carved statue and drapery of white marble with a fine effect. The country round the Seven Stars is perfectly flat, and devoted to the growth of rice, fish, and lotus plants. In a large pond beneath the temple a water buffalo is feeding on the floating leaves of lilies, while its calf calmly swims beside the mother, now and again resting its head upon her quarter. One realizes how large a part the water buffalo plays in Chinese economy, for without it the cultivation of rice would be seriously curtailed. The buffalo ploughs the inundated field, wading in the mud literally up to its belly, when no other animal could draw the primitive plough through the deep mud. In the town of Sui-hing excellent pewter work is made, and here also are fashioned various articles from the white marble of the Seven Stars, the carving of which shows excellent workmanship.

West of Sui-hing lies the city of Wuchow, where the Fu-ho River joins the West River. Once a suspension bridge existed over the Fu-ho, and two cast-

51

iron pillars about nine feet high and twelve inches in diameter are still standing, and have stood for several centuries. The pillars have both been welded at about four feet from the ground. I do not know if cast-iron can now be welded; if not, it is a lost art that certainly was known to the Chinese.

Below Wuchow, on the right bank of the river, is a district that will one day attract the big game sportsman. Here the tigers are so plentiful and so dangerous that the inhabitants do not dare to leave their homes after four or five o'clock in the afternoon. Farther down, on the left bank, is one of the most important Buddhist monasteries in China—Howlick—which accommodates about two hundred monks, and can take in an equal number of guests, who at certain seasons retire to the monastery for rest and reflection. It is situated about two miles from the river at an elevation of fifteen hundred feet. Approached by a steep pathway, at the entrance of which stand or sit two grey-robed monks armed with spears so as to be able to repel bad characters, and which as it approaches the monastery is formed into long flights of steps, Howlick is built upon a terraced plateau in the midst of primeval forest and close by a most picturesque gorge. The monastery is the resort of a large number of pilgrims, and Buddhist services take place daily in the temple, which, unlike most temples in China, is perfectly clean and well appointed.

When I visited it the service was being intoned in strophe and antistrophe, the chanters at each recurrent verse kneeling and touching the ground with their foreheads. The only accompaniment was drums and gongs, the time being marked by tapping a wooden drum of the Buddhist shape, but all was very subdued. One monk played two or three gongs of different sizes, one being only about six inches in diameter. The two long tables on which the books of the readers were placed were loaded with cakes and fruit. The fronts were hung with rich embroideries. Such a service is paid for by the pilgrims, who receive the food placed upon the tables and distribute it to their friends.

I had subsequently a long conversation with the abbot, who was most kind and hospitable. He said the monks had their own ritual, and so far as I could see Howlick is an independent community. In the monastery were many shrines, at each of which was a regular sale of sticks, beads, etc., in which a roaring trade was being done by the monks. In the lower reception room was a number of women, who purchased prayers written by a monk while they waited. For each prayer they paid from sixty cents to a dollar.

The difference in the level of the West River in the wet and dry seasons is about forty feet in its narrow parts. As the waters recede a considerable amount

of land is left on the banks available for
cultivation and enriched by the deposit
from the heavily laden flood waters. These
river borders are not allowed to lie idle, for
as the river recedes they are carefully
cultivated, and crops of vegetables and
mulberry leaves taken off before the next
rising of the waters. The river banks are then a
scene of great activity. In the district about
Kumchuk, in which sericulture is a considerable
industry, the banks of the river are all planted
with mulberry, which ratoons annually and bears
three crops of leaves, at each stripping six or
seven leaves being left at the top. The worms
are fed at first on finely shredded leaves, which have
to be changed at least twice daily, the minute young
worms being removed to the fresh leaves with the
end of a feather. The worms begin to spin in thirty-
seven days and continue spinning for seven days.
Along the river are many apparently wealthy towns,
some showing by a perfect forest of poles like masts
with inverted pyramids near the top that a large
number of the inhabitants had successfully passed
the examinations and received degrees, which
entitled them to raise these poles as an honorific
distinction before their houses. All mandarins have
two such poles erected in front of their yamens.

The West River is at present the principal

approach to the province of Yunnan, from which province and from the western portions of Kwangsi a large cattle trade is water-borne to Canton and Hong Kong. From time to time these supplies are intercepted by the river pirates, who sometimes meet their deserts. On one occasion the inhabitants of a certain town, incensed at the murder of one of their people, turned out *en masse* and followed the piratical boat down the river, firing upon her until every one of the robber gang was killed.

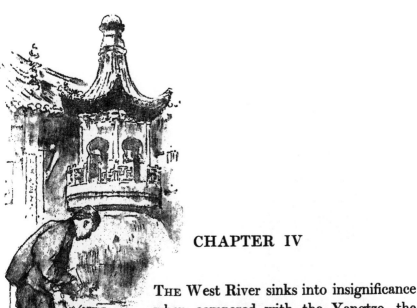

CHAPTER IV

THE West River sinks into insignificance when compared with the Yangtze, the great river over which is carried the greater portion of the commerce of China. From Wusung, the port of Shanghai, to Hankow —six hundred miles inland—battleships can be navigated, and some direct foreign trade is carried on by the cities upon its banks, though Shanghai is the great centre of foreign trade for all the Yangtze region. The history of the Yangtze is given annually by that most complete and interesting epitome of statistical knowledge—the returns of trade and trade reports by the various Commissioners of the Imperial Maritime Customs. Here everything is dealt with that bears upon the general condition of the country, and one can read at a glance the causes of fluctuations in supply, demand, and prices. In one

A SUMMER HOUSE

report we read that production was interfered with by rebellion following a drought. The insurgents, to the number of ten thousand, had armed themselves with hollowed trees for guns, and jingals as well as swords and spears. In the first encounters the insurgents got the better of the Government "troops," who were probably of the ancient type, but on the appearance of two thousand foreign drilled troops they were dispersed. The hollowed trees that did duty for guns was a device not uncommon in old China. The same substitute for cast-iron was tried by the Philippine insurgents in the uprising against Spain; but they had taken the precaution of adding iron rings. They had also large numbers of wooden imitations of Snider rifles, beautifully made, that must have looked formidable, so long as no pretence was made to shoot. The jingal is still in common use in remote districts in China, and was used against our troops in the slight engagements that took place when, under agreement with the Imperial Chinese Government, we proceeded to take over the leased territory of Kowloon. It is a matchlock, the barrel being ten feet long and the bore one inch. In the event of the spherical ball finding its billet, the wound would be of no light matter; but the chances in favour of the target are many, for the jingal requires three men for its manipulation, two of whom act as supports for the barrel, which rests on their shoulders, while the third primes the pan and manipulates the match. When the gun is fired, and the crew of three recover from the shock, it is carried to the rear for reloading, an operation that cannot be performed in a hurry. In the event of a rapid retreat the jingal remains to become the spoil of the captor. At short range, and used against a crowd, a number of jingals would probably be effective, and would present a formidable appearance; but the heroic days of short ranges, waving flags, cheering masses, and flashing steel have passed, and the trained soldier of to-day looks to his sights and to his cover.

If one could follow the ramifications of our trade through the coast ports and rivers and creeks of China, the various products of cotton and velvets, woollen goods, copper, iron, tinned plates, cement, dyes, machinery, oil, railway materials, pepper, sugar, and tea dust, with a host of other things, what an immense mass of useful and interesting information one would acquire. From the ship to the junk, from the junk to the boat, from the boat to the wheelbarrow, or the mule, and, lastly, to the toiling coolie, who alone can negotiate the dizzy paths of the more remote villages, or the frail means of transport over the raging torrents of the mountain districts. I have said that seaweed is almost unknown on the Chinese coast, and, curiously enough, seaweed is imported in considerable quantities, being used as a food, as in Ireland. The rock seaweed (called dillisk) and carrageen moss are used. For these imports are exchanged a long list of commodities, including eggs, hides (cow and buffalo), skins of all animals (from ass to weazel), silk, tea, tobacco, wood, sesamum, and opium, the latter, mainly from the provinces of Shensi, Szechwan, and Yunnan, being among the most important of the exports. I find on looking over the annual returns of trade for the Yangtze ports for 1906, that the imports of opium for the year amounted to sixty-two thousand one hundred and sixty-one piculs, while the quantity exported amounted to six hundred and forty-three thousand three hundred and seventy-seven piculs. It would be interesting to know if the arrangement entered into by the British Government, that the export of opium from India shall diminish by one-tenth annually until it has ceased, is reciprocal, in so far that not alone shall the exports of the drug from China be diminished in the same proportion, but the area under poppy cultivation be similarly controlled. If no such arrangement has been made, China will have once more demonstrated her astuteness in dealing with unconsidered outbursts of European sentiment. The statements made from time to time by anti-opium

59

enthusiasts have been made in all sincerity, and generally with a desire to approach accuracy as nearly as possible ; but, nevertheless, they are merely general statements, made under no authority of reliable statistics, and not seldom unconsciously coloured by an intense desire to emphasize an evil that they consider it impossible to exaggerate. But while it would be extremely difficult to examine systematically into the actual state of opium consumption and its effects upon the population as regards moral degradation and physical deterioration in any Chinese district, these inquiries have been made and reliable statistics obtained in Hong Kong and Singapore, and calculations based on the known consumption of opium in China have been made by competent persons, the result being to show that the statements so loosely made as to the destructive effects of opium-smoking in moderation are not borne out on close examination. My own observation of the Chinese in Hong Kong—a practically Chinese city where every man was free to smoke as much opium as he could afford to purchase—tallies with the conclusion of the exhaustive inquiries since undertaken by order of the home Government. The mass of the Chinese population are very poor, and can support themselves and their families only by incessant labour. When the day's work is done, the coolie who indulges in opium—a very small percentage of the whole—goes to an opium shop, where, purchasing a small quantity of the drug, he retires to a bench or couch, sometimes alone, sometimes with a friend, in which case they lie down on either side of a small lamp and proceed to enjoy their smoke, chatting the while. The pipe is a peculiar shape, looking like an apple with a small hole scooped in it, and stuck on the mouth orifice of a flute. Taking with a long pin looking like a knitting-needle a small quantity (about the size of a pea) of the viscous-prepared opium from the box in which it is sold, the smoker roasts it over the flame of the small lamp until it is of a consistency fit to be placed in the bowl of the pipe, on the outer portion of which the pellet has been kneaded during the heating process. Then placing the bowl to the flame, two or three deep whiffs are taken and swallowed, which exhausts the pellet, when the bowl is cleared out and the process repeated until a state of dreamy slumber or complete torpor is reached, on awaking from which the smoker leaves the place.

When one remembers the exhausting nature of coolies' work in a seaport town it is clear that if opium were smoked to excess the results would be apparent in opium-sodden loafers and beggars; but the contrary is the case, for in no town on earth is the population more efficient and industrious.

A valuable report has lately been issued by the Commission appointed by the governor, to whom the following questions were referred.

(1) The extent to which excessive indulgence in the smoking of opium prevails in the Straits Settlements.

(2) Whether the smoking of opium

    (*a*) in moderation

    (*b*) in excess

has increased in the said Settlements.

(3) The steps that should be taken . . . . to eradicate the evils arising from the smoking of opium in the said Settlements.

The Commission included a bishop, three members of the Legislative Council, including the Chinese member, and three independent gentlemen. They examined seventy-five witnesses, including every class in the population, twenty-one of whom were nominated by the anti-opium societies, and presented a report of three hundred and forty-three paragraphs, from which I cull the following excerpts.

> Par. 76. We are firmly convinced that the main reason for taking to the habit of smoking opium is the expression among the Chinese of the universal tendency of human nature to some form of indulgence.

> Par. 77. The lack of home comforts, the strenuousness of their labour, the severance from family association, and the

absence of any form of healthy relaxation in the case of the working classes in Malaya, predispose them to a form of indulgence which, both from its sedative effects and in the restful position in which it must be practised, appeals most strongly to the Chinese temperament.

Par. 91. In the course of the inquiry it has transpired that life insurance companies with considerable experience of the insurance of Chinese lives are willing, *ceteris paribus,* to accept as first-class risks Chinese who smoke two chees (116 grains) of chandu a day, an amount that is by no means within the range of light smoking, and we are informed that these insurance companies are justified in taking these risks. It appears therefore that, in the view of those remarkably well qualified to judge, the opium habit has little or no effect on the duration of life, and there is no evidence before us which would justify our acceptance of the contrary view.

Par. 96. We consider that the tendency of the evidence supports us in the opinion we have formed, as the result of our investigations, that the evils arising from the use of opium are usually the subject of exaggeration. In the course of the evidence it has been pointed out to us that it is difficult even for a medical man to detect the moderate smoker, and it is improbable that the moderate smoker would obtrude himself upon the attention of philanthropists on whose notice bad cases thrust themselves. The tendency of philanthropists to give undue prominence to such bad cases, and to generalize from the observation of them, is undoubtedly a great factor in attributing to the use of opium more widely extended evils than really exist.

Par. 106. The paralysis of the will that is alleged to result from opium-smoking we do not regard as proved, many smokers of considerable quantities are successful in business, and there is no proof that smokers cannot fill positions of considerable responsibility with credit and reliability.

Referring to statements made that the dose must inevitably be constantly increased, the report observes as follows in

Par. 112. We have, further, evidence given in many concrete cases that the dose has not been increased during considerable periods, and we have the remarkable absence of pauperism that should be strikingly prevalent if the theories mentioned above were reasonably applicable to local indulgence in opium.

On the question of enforcing prohibitive legislation, the report observes in

Par. 133. The poppy is at present cultivated in India, China, Turkey, and Persia, and it may, we consider, be assumed that short of universal suppression of the cultivation effectively carried out, prohibition in one would lead to extended cultivation in others.

The report goes on to deal with the substitution of morphia for opium as demanding the gravest consideration, its effects being infinitely more deleterious than the smoking of opium.

It will be interesting to see how the International Commission that has recently met at Shanghai has dealt with the question. The Imperial Chinese Government has issued drastic regulations, and an Imperial edict has decreed that the growing of the poppy and the smoking of opium shall cease; but the people of China have a way of regarding Imperial edicts that clash with their customs as pious aspirations. If it succeeds, it will have effected a change more complete than any that

A QUIET GAME OF DRAUGHTS.

has taken place since the adoption of the shaved head and the queue at the command of the Manchu conquerors.

The proportion of the volume of trade under the various foreign flags shows of late years a considerable diminution of our trade and an increase of that carried in German bottoms ; but this difference in the supply of commodities, while it shows a loss to our shipping, is more apparent than real as regards the commodities themselves. For the last half century or more a large quantity of cotton and other goods ordered through British houses was procured in Germany and shipped from English ports. But with the passing of the Merchandise Marks Act, a change was soon observed. When the astute Chinese trader saw printed upon his cotton cloth the advertisement that it was made in Germany, he asked the German Consul about it, and concluded that it would be better business to order it from the maker direct, which he did. The equally astute German arrived at the conclusion that as this large direct trade had developed it would be well to build the ships to carry it under its own flag, and save the transport and turnover in England. The result was a great increase of German shipping to the East, and with the increase of German argosies came the proposal, as a natural sequence, that a German navy

9   65

should be created to ensure their protection. Thus
the Act that was hailed with such appreciation
became the greatest and most valuable advertisement
ever given by one nation to another, and German
technical knowledge, thoroughness, and business
capacity have taken full advantage of the situation.
Ten years ago the German flag in Hong Kong
harbour was comparatively infrequent. To-day the
steamers of Germany frequently outnumber our
own in that great port.

The life of town and country is more sharply
divided in China than in Europe, for the absence
of local protection drives all wealthy men to the
security of the walled towns and cities. The aspect
of all the great cities south of the Yangtze is pretty
much the same, and there is not much difference in
the life of the communities. The cities are encircled
by walls about twenty-five feet high and from fifteen
to twenty feet on top, with square towers at intervals,
and great gateways at the four cardinal points. The
north gate at Hangchow, at the extremity of the
Grand Canal, is the most beautiful that I have seen
in China. Eight stone monoliths supported an
elaborate structure of three stories narrowing to the
summit that was finished by a boat-shaped structure
with ornamental ends and a curved roof. Every
portion of the great structure of stone was beautifully
carved, the upper portions being perforated. The

carved work was exquisite, figures standing in bold relief, and flowers and foliage being undercut so that a stick could have been passed behind them. The walls of Nanking and Suchow are each thirty-six miles in circumference, but within the walls are large areas that have probably never been built over. The vacant spaces may always have been used for agricultural purposes, the crops enabling the inhabitants to withstand a siege. Many of the splendid buildings of these old cities have disappeared or are now in ruins, but here and there the tiled roofs, beautiful in their curved design and brilliant glaze of green or yellow enamel, remain to testify to the innate artistic feeling of the Chinese people. The Ming tombs at Nanking, with the mile-long approach through a double row of elephants, camels, chitons, horses, etc., each ten and a half feet high and carved from a single block, are monuments that, unlike the great bronze astronomical instruments that erstwhile adorned the walls of Peking, no conquering host could carry away. On the back of each of the elephants is a heap of stones, every Chinese who passes feeling it a religious duty to wish, generally either for wealth or a son, when he casts up a stone. If it remains, the answer is favourable; if not, he continues his course in sadness, but not without hope. The porcelain tower of Nanking has disappeared, but the bronze summit, fifteen feet in diameter, remains on its site.

Inside the city walls the streets are narrow and sometimes filthy. Smells abound, but Chinese are apparently oblivious to what we consider offensive smells; and from a hygienic point of view it is certain that foul smells are better than sewer-gas, which, though it cannot be characterized as dirt, is decidedly matter in the wrong place.

Peking is unlike any of the southern cities. Its streets are wide, and the mixture of peoples from the north gives variety and colour to the street scenes. Here one meets long strings of laden camels bearing their burdens from Mongolia, and issuing grumbling protests as they follow the bell of their leader. Peking carts with richly ornamented wheels but no springs ply over the raised centre of the broad but filthy streets, the mud of winter and the dust of summer assuaging the jolting of the picturesque but uncomfortable vehicles. Sometimes in the carts are richly apparelled ladies, who are attended by mounted servants. Now and again may be seen immense funeral biers bright with red lacquer and gilding, and resting upon a platform of bamboos large enough to admit from twenty to fifty or sixty bearers. Should the funeral be that of a high official, as many as a hundred bearers are sometimes engaged. This is a form of ostentation impossible in the narrow streets of the southern cities. Peking is really four cities within the immense outer walls, which are fifty feet high and probably thirty or forty feet broad on top. On the portion of the wall commanding the legations some of the hardest fighting of the siege took place. The Temple of Heaven and the Temple of Agriculture are situated to the right and left of the south gate of the outer wall. Each temple stands in a park, and in the one the Emperor on the first day of the Chinese New Year offers a sacrifice on the great white marble terrace, and prays for blessings upon all his people, while in the Temple of Agriculture the Emperor, attended by all the great officials, attends on the first day of spring for the performance of the ceremonies, as laid down by ancient custom. This ceremony in honour of the opening of spring is one of the principal functions of the year. The Emperor, with all the Court, attends at the Temple of Agriculture in state to plough a furrow. The buffalo that draws the plough is decorated with roses and other flowers, and the plough is covered with silk of the Imperial yellow. The ground has been carefully softened, and a hard path arranged on which the Emperor walks while he guides the plough, before doing which he removes his embroidered jacket and tucks up the long silk coat round his waist, as a carpenter does when he wants to get his apron out of the way and leave his legs free. After his Majesty has ploughed his furrow, three princes, each with a buffalo and plough decorated with red silk, plough each three furrows, followed by nine of the principal officials, whose ploughs and buffaloes are decorated like those of the princes. A rice is then sown called the red lotus, which when reaped is presented as an offering— half on the altar at the Temple of Agriculture, half on that before the tablets of the Imperial family in the royal ancestral hall.

This ceremony is of very ancient date, and indicates the high position held by the agriculturist in the estimation of the Chinese. In the books of Chow, written probably about 1000 B.C., in writing against luxurious ease, it is written, " King Wăn dressed meanly, and gave himself to the work of tranquillization and to that of husbandry."

To Peking, as the centre of Chinese official life, flock all the higher mandarins from time to time, each high official—viceroy, governor, or taotai, or lower ranks—to give an account of their steward- ship at the expiration of their term of office, and to solicit a renewed appointment. Should a viceroy have acquired, say, three millions of dollars during his three years' term of office, it will be necessary for him to disburse at least one million in presents to various palace officials before he can hope for an audience and for further employment. Many of the officials put their savings into porcelain rather than invest them in speculation, or deposit them in savings banks. Some of this porcelain is buried or concealed in a safe place, and when the owner requires money he disposes of a piece. It is thought in England that great bargains of valuable porcelain can be picked up in any Chinese town. This is a mistake. Of course, great bargains may possibly be picked up anywhere, but good porcelain is highly valued in China as in Europe. Shown a very fine vase by the principal dealer in curiosities of Peking, he quoted the price at seventeen thousand dollars. The result of the Chinese custom of buying porcelain as a savings bank investment, and its re-sale when money is required, is a constant traffic in good porcelain, which can generally be procured, at its full value.

CHAPTER V

THE peasant cultivator of China spends a life of intermittent industry. In the north there is but one annual crop, but in the south two crops are grown. The principal cultivation being rice, he is perforce constrained to the system of co-operation, as, there being no fences, all the rice crop of a large flat area, sometimes minutely subdivided, must be reaped at the same time, so that when the crop has been removed the cattle and buffaloes may roam over the flat for what pasturage they can pick up before the flooding of the land and preparation for the next crop.

In the event of any farmer being late with his sowing, he must procure seed of a more rapidly growing kind, some kinds of rice showing a difference of a month or more in the time that elapses from sowing to reaping. But even when the crop is down and growing, no grass that may

be found on the edges of the paths or canals
is allowed to go to waste. Small children
may then be seen seated sideways on the
broad backs of the buffaloes while the
beasts graze upon the skirting pasture,
the children preventing them from injuring
the growing crops.

The first crop is sown about April and reaped
early in July, the second late in July and reaped
at the end of September. After the rice, which has
generally been sown very thickly in a nursery, has
been transplanted to the flooded fields and taken
root, the ground is gone over and the mud heaped
with the feet around each plant. The ground is
manured when the rice is about a foot high with
pig manure, mixed with lime and earth, and
scattered by hand at a time when the water is
low. If the crop looks poor the manure is carefully
applied round each plant, and sometimes if it is still
very backward, when the water is around it, the
manure is poured over it in a liquid state. The
water is kept on the rice field until a very short time
before reaping, and after the crop is in full ear the
Chinese like to have three days' rain, which they say
improves the yield very materially.

When the rice is six or eight inches over the
water, which is then about three inches deep, large
flocks of ducks and geese may be seen feeding on the

frogs, etc., to be found in the paddy fields (paddy is the term for rice before it has been husked), attended by a man or boy, who carries a long bamboo pole with a bunch of bamboo leaves tied at the top. When the evening comes a shake of his pole brings all the flock, sometimes numbering hundreds, out of the field, and as they emerge on the path the last duck or goose receives a whack of the bunch of leaves. It is amusing to see how this is realized by the birds, who waddle along at top speed to avoid being last. Once on the path the herd goes in front, and, placing his pole against the base of a bank, all the flock jump over it, being counted as they go. Ducks are reared in amazing numbers in Southern China, the eggs being hatched in fermenting paddy husks. Every country shop has displayed a number of dried ducks, the fowl being cut in half and spread out under pressure. But as articles of food nothing comes amiss; rats are dried in the same way and sold, though the house rat is not usually eaten, the rat of commerce being the rodent found in the rice fields. Besides rice, the farmer grows crops of rape, fruit, and a large quantity of vegetables. Mulberry trees are the main crop in the silk regions, and in the provinces bordering the Yangtze tea is produced, while to the westward the cultivation of the poppy assumes large proportions In the economy of the Chinese farmer the pig plays as prominent a part as in Ireland, for the pig is a save-all, to which all scraps are welcome. The Chinese pig is usually black. It has a peculiarly hollow back, the belly almost trailing on the ground, and it fattens easily. A roast sucking-pig is always a *pièce de resistance* at a feast.

The Chinese farmer is thrifty, but he has his distractions in card-playing and gambling in various ways that could only be devised by Chinese ingenuity. He loves a quail fight or a cricket fight, the latter being an amusement that sometimes brings a concourse of thousands together. A large mat-shed is erected and in this is placed the cricket pit. The real arena of the fight is a circular bowl with a flat bottom about seven inches in diameter. Two crickets being placed in it are excited to fury by having their backs tickled by a rat's bristle inserted in the end of a small stick, such as a pen handle. The rival crickets fight with great fury until one turns tail and is beaten. Many thousands of dollars are wagered at times upon these contests, and the most intense excitement prevails. When a man has been fortunate enough to capture a good fighting cricket he feeds it on special meal. Such a known cricket sometimes changes hands for a considerable sum. After all, the value of a cricket, like a race-horse, is what it may be able to win. As the initial expense

of a cricket is only the trouble of catching it, this is a
form of excitement within reach of the poorest, and
the villager may have in gambling for a cash (the
tenth part of a cent) as much excitement as the
richer town-dweller who wagers in dollars.

The farmer's house is not luxurious in its furniture,
but it is sufficient for his wants. With the exception
of the table almost everything is made of bamboo,
which, with the aid of fire and water, can be bent to
any shape, but there is great diversity in the lamp of
pottery or pewter or brass, the latter being somewhat
similar in shape to the ancient Roman lamp. The
bed is simply a flat board, over which a grass or palm
leaf mat is laid. The pillow is a half round piece of
pottery about ten inches long and four inches high.
A common form is that of a figure on hands and
knees, the back forming the pillow. The careful
housewife places her needlework inside the pillow,
which makes an effective workbasket. In winter the
pottery pillow is replaced by one of lacquer
and leather, which is not so cold. Over his
door will be found a beehive, made of a drum
of bamboo two feet long by twelve inches in
diameter and covered with dried clay, while
his implements of husbandry—consisting of a
wooden plough of the same shape as may be
seen on Egyptian ancient monuments, and
which with the harness he carries on his

76

shoulder to the field, a hoe, and a wooden "rake" of plain board to smooth the mud on which the rice will be sown—can be accommodated in the corner. He is not very clean and has a lofty contempt for vermin ; but sometimes he will indulge in the luxury of a flea-trap, made of a joint of bamboo three inches in diameter, the sides cut out, leaving only enough wood to preserve the shape. This he carries in his sleeve, but what he inserts as a trap I have not been able to discover.

Apart from his gambling his distractions are a visit to the temple before or after crop time, a marriage, a funeral, a procession, or a pilgrimage to one of the seven holy mountains of China. He has not often more than one wife, who, being entirely at his mercy, rules him with a rod of iron, and to whom as a rule he leaves the emotional part of the religion of the family. To her falls all the anxious care of the children, and horrible fears assail her lest the evil spirits, against whose machinations all the ingenuity of her religious superstitions is exerted, should get possession of any of her boys. To this end she will dress the boys as girls, and indulge in make-believes that would not puzzle the silliest devil that ever tormented a Chinese mother. Nor does she neglect religious duties, for she will be seen in the temple praying devoutly, and then taking up the two kidney-shaped pieces of wood, flat on one side and round on the other, that are found on the altar before the god, she will place the flat sides together between her palms and flinging them up observe the position in which they fall. If both flat sides come up, it is good; if the round, then it is evil; if one of each, there is no answer. This she repeats three times; or going to a bamboo in which are a number of canes, each bearing a number, she shakes it, as Nestor shook the helmet of Agamemnon, until one falls out, when she looks for the corresponding number among a quantity of yellow sheets of paper hung upon the wall where she reads the mystic answer to her prayer.

It is not easy for the casual inquirer to understand the religious beliefs of the Chinese. In many ways intensely materialistic, the people have a living faith, at least in reincarnation or recurring life; and while their spiritual attitude is rather a fear of evil demons than a belief in a merciful God, yet there is among them a spirit of reverence and of thankfulness for favours received. One day at Chekwan Temple—a very fine and richly ornamented temple on the Pearl River—I saw a fisherman and his family enter with a basket of fish and some fruits, which he laid upon the altar. Then, first striking the drum to call the attention of the god, the family prayed devoutly, while the father poured a libation seven times upon the altar. I asked the priest what it meant, and he answered that the man had had a good take of fish the previous night and was returning thanks. Sometimes when a member of the family is ill they will go to the temple and have a prayer written, then burning the paper, they take home the ashes, and administer them as a medicine. Again, in a temple in Canton one pillar is covered with paper figures of men, which are tied to the pillar upside down. Asking the meaning I was told that these were tied on by the light-o'-loves of young Chinese who, having taken a wife, had put an end to the temporary arrangements as common in a Chinese city as in the centres of Western civilization. The abandoned ones vainly hoped that by timely incantations and tying on of the figures their protectors might be induced to return to them. But the great annual excitement to the peasant under normal conditions is the theatrical performance that takes place in every district. The company brings its own theatre, an enormous mat-shed erection capable of accommodating an audience of a thousand people. This is erected in a few days, and for a week or more historical or social plays are performed. The actors make up and dress upon the stage, on which the more prominent members of the audience are sometimes accommodated. All the actors are men, as women are not allowed to perform; but the men who take women's parts could not be distinguished

from females, and some are very highly
paid. The dresses are very gorgeous.
In historical plays all the actors wear long
beards and moustaches which completely
cover the mouth. The bad character of
the play is always distinguished by
having the face darkened and with a
white patch on the nose. The play is
in the form of an opera in which the
singers intone their parts in a simple
recurring time, being accompanied in
unison by a couple of stringed instruments of curious form; but when an
important entry is made or one of the oft-
recurring combats take place, large cymbals
clash with deafening noise. This is never
done while the singing dialogue is proceeding.
The properties are in a large box on the stage.
If an actor is going over a bridge the attendants,
who are moving about, place a table with a
chair at either side, put over it a cloth, and
the bridge is complete. The actor walks over and
the table is removed. Should he mount a horse,
or get into a chair, conventional movements convey
the fact to the audience. In the combats one man is
always slain. Then the attendant walks forward and
drops a roll of white paper or cloth before him,
when the slain man gets up and walks out. In

Japan matters are somewhat differently done. There are always two attendants in black with wide flowing sleeves, who are supposed to be invisible. When a character is slain one stands in front, spreads his arms, and the defunct walks off, the invisible attendant moving after him, keeping between him and the audience.

In social plays the actors are no longer in gorgeous historic costumes, but are clad in modern dress. When a very poor man came on he indicated his poverty by making the movements of cracking vermin on his clothes between his nails.

It is singular how little one misses the scenery, and the audience takes the keenest interest in the plays, sometimes being moved to tears at the tragic parts.

The position of the actor is very low in the Chinese scale, no actor or child of an actor being permitted to present himself for public examination ; the brotherhood of the sock and buskin is a very large community.

When the play is finished, if there are wealthy men present servants come in laden with strings of copper cash, which are laid upon the stage.

But these are the incidents of country life in normal times. When rains are short and rivers run low, and the rice crop fails, then gaunt famine stalks over the arid land, and discontent and misery are apt to lead to grave local troubles, the people looking upon such a visitation as a direct intimation that the Emperor, as represented by the local officials, had incurred the displeasure of heaven and lost the confidence of the gods. This feeling makes for rebellion, and rebellion in China, when it is faced by Government, is dealt with in a manner so ruthless as to make one shudder.

In 1903 a famine with the usual concomitants developed in the province of Kwangsi, and harrowing descriptions of the condition of affairs came to Hong Kong, where a relief committee was formed at once. An official was sent up on behalf of the committee to inquire and report, and on his return he gave an account of what he had seen. A troublesome rebellion had broken out, and in the course of its suppression many prisoners had been taken. These wretches, with large numbers of criminals, were being executed, a general gaol delivery being thus effected, the magistrate holding that as there was not enough food for honest people none could be spared for criminals. The starving population had been reduced to such extremity that they were eating the bodies. At the same time the authorities and the gentry were doing everything in their power to relieve the suffering of the people; but all were miserably poor, and no taxes were being collected. The Hong Kong Relief Committee's representative, who had taken a first consignment of rice with him, was offered every facility by the magistrate, who not alone gave him a guard, but sent a launch to tow the rice junk up the river, sending a guard with it. The state of brutality to which the community had been reduced was shown by the following occurrence related to the representative by one of his guards, who told the story with an evident feeling that the incident redounded to the credit of the "party of order." A short time before, information having reached the local authority of the whereabouts of a "robber family," a party, including the narrator, went to the village and seized the entire family. The man they cut open, took out the entrails, cooked and ate them in the presence of the dying wretch. They cut the breasts off the woman, cooked and ate them in the same way. The woman he described as sobbing during the operation. The two were then killed. As the "soldiers" did not care to kill the children themselves, they handed knives to a number of surrounding children, who hacked the little ones to death.

This is a lurid story, but the sequel shows that even in China danger lurks in too ferocious exercise of despotic power, however well intended. The magistrate was unceasing in his efforts to cope with the famine, with the added troubles of a rebellion, in fighting which the advantage was not always with his troops. Rice was being poured into the famine districts by committees established in Hong Kong and Canton, and every assistance that could be given was afforded to them by the magistrate, who was an educated gentleman and apparently full of pity for the famishing people. His unvarying civility to the working members of the Hong Kong committee who were engaged in the distribution was at the close of their proceedings duly and gratefully acknowledged; but the warm thanks of the committee never reached him. A new viceroy had been appointed to Canton, who, on proceeding to the famine district to make personal inquiry, found that the magistrate had not been just, but had executed as criminals innocent people, among them being a secret agent sent up by the viceroy in advance to inquire into the real state of affairs. On finding this he degraded the magistrate, who thereupon committed suicide. When one reads of the reckless ferocity with which life was taken it is astonishing that he was not put an end to by poison long before the interference of the viceroy; for poisoning is not unknown, the plant named in China muk-tong being used. It is inodorous and tasteless, but if boiled in water used for tea it is almost certain death.

The life of the coast cities where East meets West is full of interest. Every treaty port has its foreign concession, where the consuls reign supreme, and a

Western system of police and municipal arrangements is adopted. Tientsin, Shanghai, Ningpo, Fuchow, Amoy, and Canton, as well as the Yangtze ports, all have on their borders large areas over which the Chinese Government has abandoned its territorial rights, and all offences or disputes are dealt with in European magistrates' or consular courts with the exception of Shanghai, where for certain offences the cases are tried in a mixed court, under the jurisdiction of a Chinese and a European magistrate. The sudden contrast from the foreign concession at Shanghai to the Chinese city is most striking; on the one side a splendid bund along the river bank, well kept public gardens, an excellent police force (mounted and foot), broad streets in which are fine shops displaying the newest European patterns, well appointed gharries standing on their appointed ranks for hire at moderate fares, and for the poorer Chinese the ubiquitous Chinese wheel-barrow—mentioned by Milton—that is palpably the one-wheeled progenitor of the Irish jaunting-car. The axle of the barrow is in the centre, the large wheel working in a high well on either side of which are two seats. There is no weight on the handles when the legs are lifted; the barrow coolie has therefore only to preserve the balance and push. These barrows are used everywhere in the Yangtze region, and are suitable for carrying heavy loads over interior tracks too narrow for two wheels. In Shanghai they are not alone used for transport of heavy burdens, but form the usual means of locomotion for the Chinese of the labouring class who prefer the luxury of driving to walking. In the morning, as in the evening, when going to work or coming from it, as many as six people may be seen sitting three a side and being pushed along by one coolie with apparent ease, or now and again one or two men on one side are balanced by a large pig tied on the other.

Along the river front, where the bund is prolonged into Chinese territory, the Western influence is seen in the police arrangements, Chinese police, or "lukongs," being similarly attired as their Chinese brethren in the "Settlements." But inside the walls the scene changes, and the Chinese city is found, simple but not pure, as Shanghai city is among the very dirtiest in all China. Yet it has its picturesque and somewhat imposing spots near the great temples. Outside the city bounds is the usual burial-place, on the border of the flat plain that surrounds Shanghai. Here the custom is to deposit the coffins on the ground, the tombs being sometimes built of brick, or the coffin being covered with thatch, while in some cases the coffins are simply left upon the ground without any covering. It must be explained that the Chinese coffin is a peculiarly solid case, built in a peculiar manner with very thick slabs of wood. In every direction are peach orchards, which when in blossom present as beautiful a sight as the famed cherry blossom of Japan. All around the plain is intersected with deep drains, the muddy bottoms of which the sporting members of the Shanghai Hunt Club now and again make involuntary acquaintance. The position of Shanghai, situated as it is near the mouth of the Yangtze, marks it out as the future emporium of the commerce of Central China, through which must ebb and flow the ever-growing trade of nine of the eighteen provinces of the Middle Kingdom. The social intercourse between the foreign and the Chinese communities is very restricted, a restriction that cannot be laid entirely at the door of either side ; but until the division becomes less clearly and sharply marked there can be no well grounded prospect of such community of feeling as will make trade relations comfortable, when the now blinking eyes of the sleeping giant have fully opened and he realizes his strength and power to command attention to his demand for reciprocal rights among the great nations of the earth.

To a foreigner the most impressive city in China is Canton, with its teeming population and intense activity. The foreign settlement of Shameen lies along the bank of the Pearl River, and on the land side is surrounded by a canal, the only entrance to the settlement being over two carefully guarded bridges. Here everything is purely Western—Western architecture, Western lawns, Western games; the flags of all the foreign nations fly over their respective consulates; and but for the Chinese domestics that one sees here and there, one might, if he turned his gaze from the river, with its maze of junks and boats of every kind, forget that he was not walking in the wealthy residential suburb of a European town. But once over the bridge and past the solid rows of stores—once the godowns of the European hongs—every trace of European influence is gone, and we enter through the city walls into a scene such as has existed in Chinese cities for centuries. The streets vary in width from six to ten feet, and are all flagged with granite slabs, and in these narrow streets is a dense mass of blue-robed Chinese, all intent upon business except when a foreigner enters into a shop to make a purchase, which always attracts a curious and observing crowd. Narrow as are the streets, the effect is still more contracted by the hanging sign-boards, painted in brilliant colours and sometimes gilt letters, that hang outside each shop. These sign-boards are sometimes ten to twelve feet long, and each trade has its own particular colouring and shape. The

A CHINESE GIRL

effect of the sign-boards, the colour of the open shops, and the gay lanterns that hang at almost every door, is very fine, and gives an idea of wealth and artistic sentiment. Every shop removes its shutters in the morning, and as there are usually no windows, the effect is that of moving through an immense bazaar, in which every known trade is being carried on, while the wares are being sold at an adjoining counter. In one shop will be found the most expensive silks and other stuffs, or rather in a row of shops, for each particular business affects certain parts of the street. Thus at one end may be a succession of shops with the most delicate and beautiful commodities, while the continuation is devoted to butchers' stalls, or fishmongers', the sudden transition being proclaimed to every sense, and outraging our feeling of the fitness of things. In the shops will be seen men at work upon the beautiful fans for which Canton is famed ; in another the shoemaker or the hatter ply their more homely trade. Tailors, stocking-makers, carpenters, blacksmiths, all are diligently at work, while here and there, poring carefully over a piece of jewellery or brass or silver work, may be seen the feather-worker attaching the delicate patterns made with the brilliant feathers of the kingfisher, the work being so minute that young men and boys only can do it, and so trying that their eyesight can only stand it for about two years. At the corners of the streets are seen tea-houses, the entire front being elaborately carved from ground to roof and glittering with brilliant gilding. Ivory-cutters carry on their trade, and jade and porcelain are displayed. A great feature in many of the streets is the bird shops, filled with singing birds or birds of brilliant plumage, of which the Chinese are very fond; wealthy Chinese gentlemen giving sometimes large sums for ivory cages for their favourites. In places the streets are covered for short distances. These gay shops are not usually found in the side streets, where the rougher trades—the butcher, the fishmonger, and the greengrocer—predominate. In these particular streets the smells are to European sense simply abominable, but appreciation or otherwise of smells is possibly a racial as well as an individual peculiarity. Among us musk is the delight of some and the horror of others.

Although too narrow for wheeled traffic, the noise of the streets is considerable, as coolies, carrying great baskets of goods or perhaps vegetables, shout panting warnings to the crowd, and all must make way for the laden coolie. Now and again a mandarin rides past, attended by his servants, or is carried in his official chair, when everybody makes way for him with

90

the most surprising alacrity. It is easy to see that the people recognize the all but despotic power that always notes the officials of a practically democratic community. The general idea that strikes a stranger when going for the first time through these narrow streets with their dense crowds is one of awe, feeling as if enmeshed in the labyrinths of a human ant-hill, from which there could be no hope of escape if the crowd made any hostile movement. But the interests of Canton are not exhausted in her crowded streets, with the marvellous absence of any jostling—the chair coolies never touching anybody with their chairs, even though they fill up half the width of the streets—for there are the various temples that have been described *ad nauseam ;* the water clock that has been going for over six centuries ; the mint, where the Government produces from time to time coins of not always clearly determined fineness; and the City of the Dead, where for a moderate payment an apartment may be engaged, in which a deceased member of a family can be accommodated until such time as the geomancer can find an auspicious position for the grave. Some of these apartments, which are all kept admirably clean, have tables on which are left the pipe of the inmate, while paper figures stand by to hand him, if necessary, the spiritual aroma of his favourite food when alive.

The guild-houses of Canton are well built and richly ornamented structures. These guild-houses are the club-houses of various provinces, or the local club of the members of different trades. Even the beggars have their guild in Canton, where strange members of that ancient and honourable profession may obtain accommodation, and permission to ply their occupation as mendicants on payment of a fee. Every beggar so licensed carries a badge, bearing which he has the right to enter a shop and demand alms. Among the procession of mandarins with their brilliant entourage who assembled to meet Liu Kun Yi, the viceroy at Nanking, on his return from Peking, in 1900, was the mandarin head of the beggars. He was arrayed in the correct and rich robes of his rank, and had his place in the procession exactly as the other mandarins, who were each surrounded or followed by their staff and their troops. The mandarin of the beggars' guild was carried in his official chair, and around him and following him was the most extraordinary and motley crowd of beggars, all in their workaday rags and tatters. Had they but arms of any sort they might have given points to Falstaff's ragged regiment. Every shopkeeper is visited at least once daily by a member of the fraternity, and whether by law or by custom he must contribute some small amount. The system is possibly a form of outdoor relief, and if one but knew its inner working it would probably be found to be a fairly satisfactory solution of a difficulty that is exercising the wits of anxious social investigators in England.

If the shopkeeper refuses to submit to the customary demand he may find a beggar, afflicted with some loathsome disease, seated at the door of his shop, where he will remain until the honour of the guild has been satisfied by a suitable donation, for there will be no stern policeman to order the persistent beggar to move on. One of the most painful sights that I have ever seen was a collection of lepers who had been allowed to take possession of a small dry patch in the middle of a deep swamp in the new territory of Kowloon. The only entrance was by a narrow path roughly raised over the swamp level. Here they had constructed huts from pieces of boxes, through which the rain entered freely. Each morning the miserable creatures dragged themselves to the neighbouring villages, the inhabitants of which charitably placed rice for them before their doors. I have never seen a more miserable collection of human beings. I had proper huts erected for them on neighbouring high ground, where at least they were free from the danger of being flooded out, and had shelter from rain and wind. There is a regular leper hospital in Canton.

It must not be assumed that Canton is entirely a

93

town of retail shops, for there are many important
factories there, some of the houses of business
covering large areas, where hundreds of men are
employed in the various manufactures.   Crowded as
is the business part of the city, one wonders that it is
not devastated by fire; but over every shop vessels
of water are kept upon the roof, ready for instant
service.   The value of land is very great, the average
value being fourteen dollars a square foot, which is
roughly about sixty thousand pounds per acre.   But
the narrow streets of Canton can be very imposing
when a high foreign official is paying a visit of
ceremony to the viceroy.   On one side of the street
is a continuous line of soldiers—the streets are too
narrow for a double line—each company with its
banner, while the other side is occupied by a dense
crowd that fills the shops and stands silently to see
the procession of official chairs go by.   The streets are
not alone swept, but carefully washed, so that they
are perfectly clean.   At each ward-gate is stationed
half a dozen men with long trumpets, like those upon
which Fra Angelico's angels blew their notes of
praise, and from these trumpets two long notes are
sounded—one high, the other low.   In the courtyard
of the viceroy's yamen is stationed a special guard of
about one hundred and fifty men, richly dressed and
carrying such arms as one sees in very old Chinese
pictures—great curved blades on long poles, tridents,

94

etc.—while thirty or forty men stand with banners of purple, yellow, blue, or red silk, each some twelve feet square, mounted on poles at least twenty feet long. The effect is singularly picturesque. The viceroy's yamen is situated more than a mile from the river, so that a large number of troops are required to line the streets. The yamen is surrounded by an extensive park, in which is some good timber. Another fine park surrounds the building once occupied by the British Consul, but now used by the cadets of the Straits Settlements and Hong Kong, who on appointment to the Colonies are sent for two years to Canton, there to study Chinese.

However busy the high official in China may be, his daily life is passed in quiet, if not in peace. With him there are no distracting sounds of street traffic, no hoot of motor-cars, no roar and rumble of motor-omnibuses, no earthquake tremors from heavy cart traffic. The streets are too narrow for this, and the yamen and the office are separated from any possible interference with business by street noises. The business of the yamen is, however, rarely done in solitude, for the yamen " runners," as the crowd of lictors and messengers are called, overrun the entire place, and the most important conversations are carried on in the presence of pipe-bearers and other personal attendants, to say nothing of curious outsiders, that almost precludes the possibility of

95

inviolable secrecy. It is possible that where foreigners are not mixed up in the matter there may not be so many anxious listeners, but there are few things about a yamen that are not known by those whose interest it is to know them.

The official proceeds with his work upon lines that have been deeply grooved by custom, and however energetic he may be, he is careful not to make violent changes, nor will he hastily leave the beaten track. As a rule, no community becomes violently agitated by inaction on the part of a government or of an official, however much it may be deprecated. In China the only fear in such a case would be from the action of the censors, who are appointed in various parts of the empire, and who have proved by their denunciation of even the highest officials for sins of omission, as well as commission, that China possesses among her officials men whose fearlessness and independence are equal to that of men of other races, whose honoured names have come down to us in song and story.

The rigid etiquette of China preserves a dignity in the conduct of all public business, and it is against the first principles of an educated Chinaman to use rough or harsh terms that would be considered vulgar. The written language is so capable of different interpretations that in treaties with China, which are generally written in three languages—

JERKS AT DINNER

Chinese, French or English—and the language of the contracting countries, it is always stipulated that in construing the terms of the treaty one of the two languages, not the Chinese, is to be taken as interpreting its true meaning. This does not necessarily infer dishonest intentions on the part of the Chinese; but the fact is that as each one of the many thousands of Chinese characters may mean more than one thing, the real meaning has sometimes to be inferred from the context, so that there are peculiar difficulties attending the close and accurate interpretation of a treaty or dispatch. It is popularly supposed that Sir Robert Hart and Sir J. McLeavy Brown are the only foreigners who have complete mastery of the art of writing Chinese so as to ensure the accurate expression of the meaning to be conveyed. The yamen of a high official, with his residence, covers a large area, as no house is built more than one story high. Such a building might by its dominating height interfere disastrously with the *fung sui* of even a city, and is always bitterly resented. The steeples of churches have something to answer for in this way in keeping alive the spirit of antagonism fostered by the daily maledictions of the Chinese, who bear patiently with submission rather than acquiescence the presence of a dominant foreign

influence that, if they have any living superstition on
the subject, must convey to them an impression of
evil.   The yamen usually consists of a series of
courtyards, off which are built the apartments for the
numerous staff as well as the private apartments of
the family, and in one of these, when the business of
the day is concluded, the official receives the visits of
his friends and smokes the calumet of peace, or plays
one of those complicated games of Chinese chess to
whose intricate rules and moves our game of chess
is simplicity itself.   Sometimes after his work he
indulges in his pipe of opium, after the manner of our
own three-bottle men of the last century.   The late
Liu Kun Yi, the able Viceroy of Nanking, who with
Chang Chi Tung, his neighbouring viceroy, kept the
Yangtze provinces quiet through the Boxer troubles
was a confirmed opium-smoker.   But one thing he
never does—he never hurries.   Haste is to him
undignified, and he eschews it.   In his official deal-
ings he will adopt methods that would not pass
muster in our courts ; but from the Emperor to the
coolie those methods are understood and accepted.
Much might be written on the ethics of what we call
official corruption; but let the facts be what they
may, the people understand the system, the Government understand it, and there is no popular demon-
stration against it.   Nor must we forget that official
" irregularity " is not unknown outside China.

TEA

The social side of the life of a Chinese mandarin is not confined to his own yamen. He is fond of visiting his friends and engaging in intellectual conversation over a friendly cup of tea—and such tea! We have no idea in Europe of the exquisite delicacy of the best Chinese tea as prepared by a Chinese host. The tea is made by himself, the leaves being only allowed to remain in the freshly boiled water for four or five minutes. It is then poured into cups of delicate porcelain, about the size of a liqueur glass, and sipped without the addition of milk or sugar. After the tea has been drunk, the aroma of the cup is enjoyed. The perfume is delicious.

CHAPTER VI

THE houses of the wealthy inhabitants are on the east side of
the city, and are separated from
the streets by high walls. On
entering the grounds, the visitor
passes through several courtyards
and reception halls, supported on beautifully carved
granite pillars, a wealthy Chinese gentleman sparing
no expense in the lavish and tasteful decoration of
his home. From the courtyards one enters the
gardens, in which there is invariably a pond in which
water-flowers—lilies, lotus, etc.—are grown, and in
which there are shoals of goldfish. A rockery is
generally added, with quaintly contrived approaches
and caverns, and a bridge over the pond leads now
and again to a small island on which a decorated
tea-house has been erected. The bridge is always
angular, like those that are seen on the old blue

100

china plates. In one large house, from which the owner was absent, were some specimens of hammered iron-work that were the very perfection of artistic workmanship. They were blades of grass, reeds, and flowers, each specimen being placed in a window between two panes of glass. These specimens of iron-work were made about four hundred and fifty years ago by an artist whose name is still held in honour. Large sums have been offered for them, but the fortunate owner holds them more precious than gold.

A great feature of Canton is its flower-boats, of which many hundreds are moored together, and form regular streets. These boats are all restaurants, and here the wealthy young Chinamen entertain each other at their sumptuous feasts. The giver of the entertainment always engages four or five young women for each guest, who sit behind the gentlemen and assist in their entertainment. As the feast is a long function, consisting of many courses, it is not necessary for the guests to be present during the entire function. Sometimes a guest will put in an appearance for one or two courses. Music is played and songs are sung, and possibly there may be ramifications of the entertainment into which one does not pry too closely; but again there are regulated customs in China openly acknowledged and less harmful than the ignored but no less existing canker that has eaten into the heart of Western civilization.

The wives and daughters of officials are in small towns at a certain disadvantage, for etiquette demands that they shall confine their visits to their social equals, who are not many. In large cities they have the ladies of the wealthy merchants to visit, and they are by no means devoid of subjects of conversation. They take a keen interest in public affairs, and exercise no small an amount of influence upon current topics. Many of the Chinese ladies are well educated, and have no hesitation in declaring their views on matters connected with their well-being. A very short time ago there was in Canton a public meeting of women to protest against an unpopular measure. One result of missionary effort in China has been the education of a large number of Chinese women of different classes in English, which many Chinese ladies speak fluently. When Kang Yu Wei, the Chinese reformer, was in Hong Kong, having taken refuge there after his flight from Peking, his daughter was a young Chinese lady who spoke only her own language. Two years later, during which time the family had resided in the Straits Settlements, this lady passed through Hong Kong, speaking English fluently. She was on her way to the United States to pursue her studies.

The movement for reform that has begun to

agitate China is by no means confined to the men. In 1900 a women's conference met in Shanghai, under the presidency of Lady Blake, to consider the question of the home life of the women of China. The conference sat for four days, during which papers were read by both European and Chinese ladies on various social questions and customs affecting all classes of the women of China. The conference covered a wide range of subjects :—Treatment of Children ; Daughters-in-law ; Betrothal of Young Children and Infants ; Girl Slavery in China ; Footbinding ; Marriage Customs ; Funeral Customs ; Social Customs ; and its proceedings contain valuable accounts at first hand of the conditions and customs of women from every part of the Middle Kingdom. The following remarks were made by the president at the conclusion of the conference.

"We have now concluded the consideration of the subjects that were selected for discussion at this conference on the ' Home Life of Chinese Women.' We have all, I am sure, been keenly interested in the excellent papers and addresses with which we have been favoured, containing so much information from all parts of this vast empire that must have been new to many of us. I regret to find that the lot of Chinese women, especially of the lower classes, appears on closer observation even less agreeable than I had thought. The hard fate of so many of the slave-girls, for example, must excite the pity and sympathy of all men and women not altogether selfishly insensible to human sufferings from which they are exempt. But while we have been gazing on a good deal of the darker side of the lives of the women and girls of China, we must not forget that shadows cannot exist without light, so there must be a bright side in life for many Chinese women, and some of the papers read have shown us that no small number of Chinese ladies, independently of European influences, extend noble-minded and practical charity to those amongst their humbler neighbours who may stand in need of such assistance. Possibly some of us may be too apt to judge the better classes of the Chinese by the standards of the lower orders, with whom as a general rule Europeans are chiefly thrown. How would the denizens of our ancient cathedral closes, or the occupants of our manor-houses at home, like foreigners to judge of them by the standard of the inhabitants of the lower stratum of our society and the waifs and strays, who too often in other lands bring the reverse of credit to their country? I cannot help hoping, likewise, that as habit becomes second nature—and that to which we are accustomed seems less dreadful, even when intrinsically as bad—

A TYPICAL STREET SCENE.

so some things that to us would make existence a
purgatory may not be quite so terrible to the women
of China as they appear to us.   I would fain hope
that even in such a matter as foot-binding there may
be some alleviation to the sufferings of those who
practise it, in the pride that is said to feel no pain.
Of the deleterious effects of the practice—physically
and mentally—there can be no doubt, and it is most
satisfactory to find that the spark of resistance to the
fashion of foot-binding has been kindled in many
parts of China.   As new ideas permeate the empire,
I have no doubt the women of China will not be
greater slaves to undesirable fashions or
customs than are the women of other lands.
The greater number of the ills and discomforts
of Chinese women, I cannot help thinking,
must be eradicated by the people of China
themselves ; all that outsiders can do is to
place the means of doing so within their
reach.   As year by year the number increases
of cultivated and enlightened Chinese ladies,
trained in Western science and modes of
thought, while retaining their own distinctive
characteristics, so will each of them prove a stronger
centre from which rays of good influence will
reach out to their country-women.   I was once
given a flower that had rather a remarkable history.
I was told that somewhere in Greece a mine had

been found that was supposed to have been worked by the ancient Greeks. Its site was marked by great heaps of rocks and refuse. The Greeks of old, great as was their genius, which in some ways exceeded that of modern days, were not acquainted with a great deal that science has revealed to us, and in examining these heaps of stones and rubbish flung out of the mine in days of old, it was found that most of it contained ore, the presence of which had never before been suspected, but which was sufficient in amount to make it worth while submitting the refuse to a process that would extract the latent wealth. So the great heaps of stone were removed, for smelting or some such process, and when they were taken away, from the ground beneath them sprang up plants, which in due time were covered with beautiful small yellow poppies of a kind not previously known to gardeners. It is supposed that the seed of the flowers must have lain hidden in the earth for centuries. May it not be like this with China? In her bosom have long lain dormant the seeds of what we call progress, which have been kept from germinating by the super-incumbent weight of ideas, which, while they may contain in themselves some ore worth extracting, must be refined in order to be preserved, and must be uplifted in order to enable the flowers of truth, purity, and happiness to flourish in the land. Two of the heaviest rubbish heaps that crush down the blossom progress are ignorance and prejudice. I trust that the conference just held may prove of use in removing them."

Whatever may be thought of the relative prudence of choosing one's own wife, or having the young lady provided by family diplomacy, as is the Eastern custom, there is no doubt that Chinese women make affectionate wives and mothers. A forlorn woman at Macao, day after day wailing along the shore of the cruel sea that had taken her fisher-husband, waving his coat over the sea, burning incense, and calling upon him unceasingly to return to her, was a mournful sight; and I have seen distracted women passing the clothes of their sick children to and fro over a brisk fire by a running stream, and calling upon the gods they worshipped to circumvent the demons to whose evil action all sickness is attributed. Indeed, the loss of the husband himself would, in the average Chinese opinion, be better for the family than the loss of an only son, as without a male descendant the ancestral worship, on which so much depends for the comfort of the departed members, cannot be carried out in proper form. That the terrors of superstition enter largely into the Chinese mind is clearly shown, but there is also present the saving grace of faith in the possibility of assuaging whatever may be considered the discomforts of the after life, and Chinese are particular in ministering to the wants of the departed. I have seen in Hong Kong two women gravely carrying a small house, tables, chairs, and a horse, all made of tissue paper and light bamboo, to a vacant place where they were reverently burnt, no doubt for the use of a departed husband. This is the same faith that raised the mounds over the Scandinavian heroes, who with their boats or war-horses and their arms were buried beneath them.

When a child is born, a boat made similarly of tissue paper and fixed on a small bundle of straw is launched upon the tide. If it floats away, all will be well ; if flung back upon the shore, there is gloom in the house, for Fortune is frowning. Or, when members of the family are lost at sea, similar boats with small figures seated in them, and with squares of gold and silver paper representing money placed at their feet, are sent adrift. Such boats are constantly to be seen floating in the harbour of Hong Kong, each one a sad emblem of poignant sorrow, with that desperate anxiety of those bereft to reach behind the veil that lies in the sub-conscious mind of all humanity.

This is the mournful aspect of Chinese life, especially among the poorer classes. But Chinese ladies, though they take their pleasures in a different manner, are no less actively engaged in the amenities of social intercourse than are their Western sisters.

Violent physical exercise does not appeal to them—
our compelling muscularity is a hidden mystery to all
Eastern people—but visiting among themselves is
constant, and the preparation for a visit, the powder-
ing and painting, the hair-dressing, and the careful
selection of embroidered costumes, is as absorbing a
business as was the preparation of the belles of the
court of *Le Roi Soleil*. To the European man the
fashion of a Chinese lady's dress seems unchanging—
a beautifully embroidered loose jacket, with long
pleated skirt and wide trousers, in strong crimson or
yellow, or in delicate shades of all colours—but
Western women probably know better, as doubtless
do the Chinese husbands and fathers, who are
usually most generous to the ladies of the family.
The general shape is unchanging, for in China it is
considered indelicate for a woman to display her
figure ; but the Chinese milliner is as careful to change
the fashion of the embroidery at short intervals as is
the French *modiste* to change the form of the robe.
Therefore there are always to be procured in the
great towns beautiful embroidered costumes in excellent order that have been discarded at the command
of tyrant fashion as are the dresses of the
fashion-driven ladies of the West.

The etiquette of the preliminaries of a visit
is as rigid as is the etiquette of all social
intercourse in China ; the scarlet visiting

card, three or four inches wide and sometimes a foot long—its dimensions being proportioned to the social position of the visitor—being first sent in, and returned with an invitation to enter, while the hostess dons her best attire and meets the visitor at the first, second, or third doorway, according to the rank of the latter, and the elaborate ceremonial on entering the room. These accomplished, the conversation follows the lines that conversation takes where ladies meet ladies all the world over. The friendly pipe is not excluded, and probably books, children, cooks, social incidents, and possibly local politics, form the media of conversation. The social customs of China do not afford much opportunity for scandal ; but who can say ? Cupid even in China is as ingenious as he is mischievous. Games, too, are indulged in, the Chinese card games being as mysteriously intricate as is their chess.

Should the guest bring her children, the little ones all receive presents, these delicate attentions being never neglected ; indeed, the giving of presents at the New Year and other annual festivals is a settled Chinese custom.

CHAPTER VII

THOUGH Hong Kong, when handed over to Great
Britain in 1841, was a practically uninhabited island,
it has now a population of 377,000, of which 360,000
are Chinese. The city of Victoria is situated round
the southern shore of the harbour, and is, next to
London, the greatest shipping port in the world.
Behind the city steep hills rise to the height of
over 1,800 feet, their rugged sides scored by well
constructed roads and dotted over with handsome
buildings, while a cable tramway leads to the Peak
(1,200 feet high), where fine houses and terraces afford
in summer accommodation for the European residents, who find in its cool heights relief from the
oppressive temperature of the sea level. It is hard
to say whether Hong Kong is more beautiful from
the harbour or from the Peak. From the one is seen
the city crowded round the shore behind the broad
praya or sea front, and sweeping up the precipitous

111

sides of the hills—spreading as it climbs from street
to terrace, from terrace to villa, up to the very Peak—
terrace and villa nestled in the everlasting verdure of
the luxuriant tropics, varied by blazes of colour
from tree, shrub, and climber, the blue masses of
hydrangea at the Peak vieing with the brilliant
masses of purple bougainvillia, or yellow alamanda
of the lower levels, the whole bathed in such sunshine
as is rarely seen in temperate regions, while above
the blue sky is flecked with light fleecy clouds.
Away to the eastward is the happy valley, a flat
oval, around which the hill-sides are devoted to a
series of the most beautifully kept cemeteries in the
world. Here Christian and Mohammedan, Eastern
and Western, rest from their labours, while below
them, in the oval valley, every sport and game of
England is in full swing.

From the Peak we look down upon the city and
the harbour, and our gaze sweeps onward over the
flat peninsula of Kowloon to the bare and rugged
hills that sweep from east to west. But the interest
centres in the magnificent harbour, on whose blue
bosom rest the great steamers of every nation trading
with the Far East, round whose hulls are flitting
the three hundred and fifty launches of which the
harbour boasts, whose movements at full speed in a
crowded harbour bear witness to the splendid nerve
of their Chinese coxwains. Out in the harbour,

towards Stonecutter's Island, the tall masts of trim American schooners may be seen, the master—probably part owner—with sometimes his wife on board, and with accommodation aft that the captains of our largest liners might envy, while the thousands of Chinese boats of all descriptions look like swarms of flies moving over the laughing waters of the bay. The hum of the city is inaudible, and even the rasp of the derricks that feed the holds of the steamships or empty them of their cargoes comes up with a softened sound, telling its tale of commercial activity.

At night the scene is still more enchanting, for spread out beneath are gleaming and dancing the thousands of lights afloat and ashore. The outlines of the bay are marked by sweeping curves of light, and the myriad stars that seem to shine more brightly than elsewhere are mirrored in the dark waters, mingling with the thousands of lights from the boats and shipping.

This is normal Hong Kong, and in the warm season, for in winter it is cold enough to demand the glow of the fire and the cheerful warmth of furs. But the beautiful harbour lashed to wild fury by the dreaded typhoon is a different sight. All may look well to the uninitiated, who wonders to see groups of sampans and lighters, sometimes twenty or more, being towed by single launches to Causeway Bay, the boat harbour of refuge; but the gathering clouds in the south-east, the strong puffy gusts of wind, and the rapidly falling barometer with the characteristic pumping action, warn the watchful meteorological staff that the time has come to hoist the warning signal, while in addition the south-easterly heave of the sea gives notice to the careful sea-captain that he had better not be caught in narrow waters except with both anchors down and a full head of steam ready.

With a blackening sky, increasing wind, and troubled sea there is no longer room for doubt, and active preparations are made ashore and afloat. While cables are lengthened, top hamper made snug, and steam got up on sea, all windows are carefully fastened with hurricane bars on shore, for should a window be blown in when the typhoon is at its height there is no knowing how far the destruction may extend, the walls being sometimes blown out and the contents of the house scattered over the hill-side. I have seen such a typhoon that reached its maximum in the early morning. The whole harbour was foaming with a devil's dance of wild waters, hidden by a thick blanket of spray, through which from time to time great waves were dimly seen dashing over the high wharf premises, or godowns, of Kowloon, while minute-guns of distress boomed from out the wrack of sea and mist, heard as dull thuds in the howling of the mighty typhoon, and calling for help that none could give. By ten o'clock the typhoon had swept on to the north, leaving scores of ships and junks sunk in the harbour, a mile of sampans smashed to pieces at the Kowloon wharves, and hundreds of victims beneath the now moderating seas, while the harbour was filled with floating bales of merchandise.

The incident was the means of demonstrating the organizing capacity of the Chinese. As soon as the sea had moderated sufficiently to allow a launch to live, I sent for a Chinese gentleman and suggested that something should be done to relieve the sufferers and rescue those who still required assistance, and found that already the guild had sent out two powerful launches, one with coffins for the drowned, the other, with a doctor on board, equipped with the necessary means of succour for the injured, and food for those who had lost their all. Steaming along the Kowloon shore an hour afterwards, where the wreckage of boats was heaving and falling in a mass of destruction twenty to thirty feet wide along the sea wall, there was no sign, as might have been expected, of stunned despair; but the crowd of boat-people, men and women, who had escaped with their lives were working with a will and as busy as bees, each endeavouring to save something from the smashed wreckage of what had been their home, the men jumping

115

from one heaving mass to another, diving betimes and struggling with the adverse buffets of fate with an energy none the less for their stoical acceptance of the inevitable.

Although Hong Kong is a British possession it is essentially a Chinese city. British supervision has seen to it that the streets are wide and all the houses well and solidly built, save a few remaining houses of the era preceding the creation of a sanitary board, and cleanliness of house and surroundings is secured by careful and unremitting inspection. The shops are a mixture of European architecture and Chinese decoration, which runs into rich and elaborate carving and gilding. Outside are hung the same pendant signs that give such colour to the streets of Canton. Blue is the predominant colour worn by all Chinese, save the sweating coolies who toil along the quays of the great port, and the blue crowd that fills the busy streets harmonizes with the surrounding colours. The splendid buildings in what are called the principal streets, where banks, hotels, and counting-houses of the important European firms are situated, with the shops that cater more especially for the wants of foreign residents and tourists, differ but little from the architecture of a European city, while the shops contain all that purchasers can require of European wares, or Chinese and Japanese products wherewith to tempt the inquiring tourist.

But the wealthiest part of the city is in the Chinese quarter, and here property has changed hands at startling figures, sometimes at a rate equal to one hundred and sixty thousand pounds an acre. Here the shops are purely Chinese, and every trade may be seen in operation, while the doctor puts up a sign that he cures broken legs, or the dentist displays a small board, from which hang five or six long strings of molars of portentous size showing every phase of dental decay. Everywhere is seen a teeming population instinct with ceaseless activity. Rickshaws rush past, these most convenient little carriages for hire having one coolie in the shafts, while private rickshaws have one or two in addition pushing behind; or the more sedate chair swings by, borne by two or four coolies, the men in front and rear stepping off with different feet so as to prevent the swinging of the chair. The shops in this quarter have abandoned the glass front and are open, save when at night they are closed by planks set up and fastened with a bar behind the last two. The shop is then secure from any attempt to break in from the outside; but cases are on record where armed robbers have slipped in at the last moment and, closing the plank which secured them from observation, produced revolvers and walked off with the contents of the till, leaving the terrified owner and his assistants bound and gagged while they made their escape.

The early life of the city is an interesting study. At five o'clock the people are astir. The working men apparently take their morning meal in the streets, where tables are erected on which are large vessels of rice, and of boiling congee (a mixture of rice flour and water), piles of vegetables of various sorts chopped fine, dishes of scraps of meat, including the uncooked entrails of fowls, pieces of fish, and relishes of soy and other sauces. The hungry customer is handed a bowl half full of rice, on which is placed small portions of the various vegetables and a piece of meat, or some scraps of entrails, over all is poured a ladle full of the boiling congee, and the repast is ready. With his chopsticks the customer, holding the bowl to his wide open mouth, shovels in nearly as much rice as it will hold, then picking from the bowl pieces of the luscious morsels with which it is garnished, he lays them on the yet untouched rice, when he closes his mouth and proceeds with the process of mastication and deglutition. Each mouthful is a course, and the same process is repeated until the morning meal is complete. Hard by may be seen a purveyor of whelks, which are a favourite food, especially with boys, who have all the excitement of gambling in satisfying their hunger. The whelks are in a basket, to the handle

118

of which a dozen pieces of wire with crooked ends are attached by long cords. A small boy appears and lays a cash upon the stall, at the same time drawing from a deep bamboo joint a bamboo slip, one of the many in the pot. At the end of the slip is a number, or a blank, and the hungry lover of chance may find the result of his first venture a blank, or he may be fortunate enough to draw a prize with a number, which represents the number of whelks that he is to receive. These he deftly picks out with one of the crooked wires. They must, of course, be consumed "on the premises," for the cautious caterer takes no chances by permitting the wire to be detached from the cord. Boys are active and unscrupulous, and crooked wires cost money. Balls of rice flour, fried in lard, are another favourite food of the streets, and sweetmeats of appalling stickiness and questionable preparation are always to be found in Chinese quarters. The morning crowd is always good-humoured, chaffing and laughing with a heartiness that explodes the European idea of Chinese stolidity and want of expression.

The Chinese workman eats but twice a day. His morning meal is between six and eight o'clock, and his afternoon meal is at four.

By this time the boats have arrived from Kowloon

with their loads of vegetables, and the small hawkers are busily carrying them from house to house for the consumption of Chinese households, while the outlying greengrocers are being supplied with their daily stock, in the setting out of which great care is exercised, the Chinese greengrocer having an artistic eye for effect. No small shop does a more flourishing business than the druggist's and herbalist's, the Chinese having faith in the use of " simples," though remedies including the calcined teeth of tigers and vertebræ of serpents are not without their moral effect, and the mystery of a pill three-quarters of an inch in diameter has yet to be fathomed. At the Chinese New Year, tied up over every door will be seen a small bundle of vegetables, consisting of five plants: the *Acorus calamus*, representing a sword, and the *Euphorbia*, a fighting-iron, to ward off evil spirits ; the onion, to guard against the spirit of malaria ; the *Artemisia vulgaris* and the *Davallia tennifolia*. This charm is as efficacious as the house leek that, in the imaginative pre-national school days, was carefully planted on the roof of Irish cottages as a sure preservative against fire.

But the busiest man in the early morning is the barber, for the Chinese workman does not shave his own head, and small crowds assemble in each barber's shop, where tongues wag freely, and some read the morning papers while awaiting their turn. However

ON A BACKWATER

great the crowd, there is no sign of hurry in the manipulation of the placid barber. Not alone is the front of the head shaved, but the eyebrows and eyelashes are attended to ; then the ears are explored and cleaned with minute care ; and, lastly, the client is massaged and shampooed while he sits bent forward, the hammering upon back and sides being by no means gentle, and ending with a resounding smack with the hollowed palm of the barber's hand. The constant manipulation of the ears is supposed to be injurious as tending to produce deafness, but without it the customer would not consider that he had value for his thirty cash, the usual fee—about one-third of a cent. The end of the operation is the plaiting of the long queue, which between the real and the false hair freely used reaches nearly to the heels, and is finished by a silk tassel plaited into the end. Sometimes a man may be seen plaiting his own queue, which he does by taking it over the rung of a ladder, and moving backwards so as to preserve the strain.

Among the skilled workmen, the sawyer and the stonecutter are most in evidence to the ordinary visitor, who is astonished to see a squared log two feet in diameter being sawn by a single man. Having got the log into position, one man with a frame-saw does the whole business. He stands on top, and the work is extremely arduous ; but an enormous amount of timber is sawn in this way The stonecutter has a lighter job. The Chinese are very expert quarrymen, and cut out by iron or wooden wedges great blocks of granite, the wedge-holes having been prepared by iron chisel-headed bolts. Wooden wedges are then driven in and wetted, the expansion of the wedge forcing out the block, which requires but little squaring, so carefully is the cleavage effected.

One generic difference between the physical formation of Western and Eastern races is the facility with which the latter can sit upon their heels. An Asiatic will sink down upon his heels with as much ease and with as restful comfort as can a European upon a chair; and in stonecutting the workman may be seen sitting upon the stone on which he is working, sometimes seated on the edge while chiselling the perpendicular side below him. In this position a row of workmen look at a distance like a row of vultures sitting upon a ledge.

The lowest form of labour in Hong Kong is the work of the coolies, who carry coals and building materials to the Peak district; and here we have a striking evidence of the patient industry and extraordinary ingenuity with which the piece-work labourer secures the largest possible amount of result from the day's labour. Up the steep hill-side every brick or basket of sand and lime that has gone to build the houses and barracks of the Peak district has been carried up in the double baskets, suspended from the bamboo carrying-pole of a working coolie, who is paid by the load. Now a heavy load, sometimes weighing a hundredweight, carried up very steep roads for two miles or so, means slow progress, with many rests. The coolie manages to reduce the intervals of rest to the smallest compass. Placing two loads together, he carries one for fifty yards and there deposits it, returning for the second, which is carried up one hundred yards. Dropping that, he—or she, for the matter of that, for the coolie hill-carriers are sometimes women, not seldom old and feeble—returns to the first load and carries the burden fifty yards beyond the second, which is in turn taken up in the same way. There is no standing idle or sitting down to rest, the only relief being that of dropping the load and walking back down hill to take up the one left behind. This system of overlapping saves all the time that otherwise must be lost in resting, as no human being could carry up a load to the Peak without frequent intervals of rest.

After the day's work is ended the workman does not affect a tavern. He dearly loves a game, or, more strictly speaking, a gamble; and while all gambling-houses are put down with a strong hand, no conceivable

123

official ingenuity could circumvent the gambling propensities of a people whose instruments of games of chance are not confined to cards or dice. The number of seeds in a melon, or any other wager on peculiarities of natural objects will do as well, and afford no damning evidence should an officious member of the police force appear. The game of chi-mooe is not confined to the working people, but is a favourite game with all classes, and the shouts and laughter that accompany it now and again bring complaints from the neighbours whose rest is disturbed. The game is simple and is played by two. One suddenly flings out his hand with one, two, or more fingers extended, at the same moment the other must guess the number. Curling has been called the roaring game, but no curler ever made a greater racket than two excited chi-mooe players. One would imagine that the guessing of the number of fingers extended must be a matter of pure chance, but a Chinese gentleman assured me that in the flinging forward of the hand there is a muscular difference in the form if one, two, three, or more fingers are to be extended, and this difference is observed with lightning rapidity by an expert player.

However content the adult Chinaman may be with sedentary amusements, the energy of youth is in full force in the Chinese schoolboy. He is rapidly acquiring a taste for European games, such as cricket and football, but he has always played the game of hopscotch, but little differing from the game played in an English village. Where a ring can be formed he also plays a game of shuttlecock, the only instrument being a cork or piece of light wood with two or three feathers to regulate its flight and fall. This is played solely with the feet, the shuttlecock being kicked from one to the other with extraordinary dexterity. The shuttlecock is often kept up for five or even ten minutes at a time, foot and eye working together with wonderful precision.

CHAPTER VIII

THERE is one sport in which the adult Chinaman shines. Each year in the month of June the boatmen and fishermen hold a festival at which the great feature is the dragon-boat races. The dragon-boat is about ninety feet long and only wide enough to admit of two men with paddles sitting side by side on each thwart. In this boat from sixty to eighty men are seated, while in the centre stands a man with a drum or gong before him on which he beats the time. A man stands at the stern with a long steering paddle, and a boy sits in front with two lines in his hands attached to a large dragon's head with which the bow is adorned, and which moves from side to side as the lines are pulled. Two contending boats paddle to the starting-buoy and at a signal they are off. The frantic encouragement of the men beating time, the

126

furious but rhythmic splash of nearly two hundred paddles in the onrushing boats, and the natural movement from side to side of the brightly coloured dragons' heads, is one of the finest and most inspiriting sights imaginable. Every muscle is strained, and no sport on earth shows for the time a more tremendous effort of muscular energy. Sometimes in the excitement of the race the boats collide, in which event the race must be run again, for the mixture of paddles makes it impossible to disentangle without a dead stop. But such a *contretemps* leads to no mischief or quarrelling. The accident is treated good-humouredly all round, and it only means another race. On the river at Canton literally thousands of boats make a line to see the races paddled. There are no police and no stewards of the course, but no boat ever attempts to break the line or cause any obstruction.

The Chinese delight in festivals and spectacular effects, in which they give proof of organizing capacity. A very striking festival was that in honour of a son of the god of war, held at Macao every tenth year in the intercalary moon. It was a guild procession—watchmakers, tailors, shoemakers, etc. Each guild had carried before it a great triangular, richly embroidered banner, also an umbrella of honour. Many had also a long piece of embroidery carried horizontally on poles. There were ornamental chairs of the usual type, some with

127

offerings to the gods, some with wooden drums. Each guild had its band ; some string bands, some reeds and gongs, some Chinese viols and mandolins, the latter being frequently played while held over the head or resting on the back of the neck. Each guild marched two and two behind the band, the members being dressed in mauve silk coats and broad red or yellow sash tied round the waist with richly embroidered ends down each leg. The watch-makers' guild all carried watches on the right breast. Children, richly dressed in mediæval costume, were mounted on caparisoned ponies, and some guilds had cars on which were allegorical groups of children. In some cases, by an ingenious arrangement of an iron frame, a child held a sword at length which, apparently, pierced another child through back and breast. The variety of these groups was very great. From time to time the procession stopped, and then the children were taken down for a rest, the iron frames being disconnected from their easily detach-able sockets. In the meantime each group was attended by men who held umbrellas over the children to protect them from the sun.

Each guild had its attendant coolies carrying stools, and when the procession stopped the members at once sat down, starting up at once on the sound of a gong that regulated the halting and starting, when the stools were taken up by the coolies.

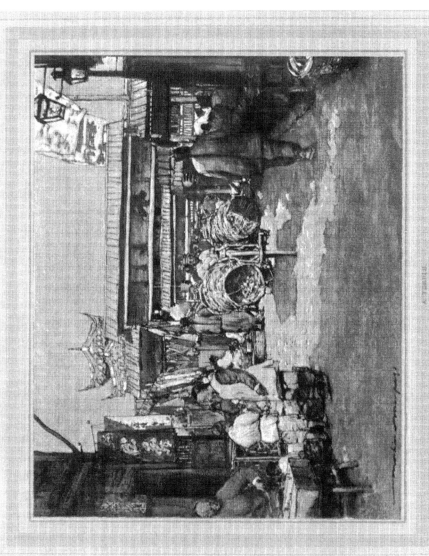

The procession finished with a dragon carried by twenty-six men. It was a hundred and forty feet long, the back of green and silver scales, the sides being stripes of red, green, pink, and yellow silk. This dragon was preceded by a man, who danced before it with a large ball representing the moon. At this the dragon made dashes from one side of the street to the other, but was staved off by another, who carried a ball surrounded by gilt rays. This probably represented the sun saving the moon from being swallowed by the dragon, as is supposed to take place in an eclipse. The dragon went along the street with sinuous rushes from side to side. Where there was room it wound round and round, but uncoiled on the touch upon its tail of the gilt ball with the golden rays. The procession took an hour and a half to pass a given point. The most perfect order prevailed, the crowd keeping a clear space. At the finish each guild went to its own district, and the decorations were carefully stowed away for future use.

Such a festival is, of course, a local holiday; but the only legal Chinese holidays are at the New Year, when all business is suspended. The viceroy puts his seal away; the governor and the magistrate follow suit; the merchant closes his place of business and squares his books, while his employees take the opportunity to

17   129

revisit their homes in the country. The shopkeeper generally has a feast for all his people, at the conclusion of which he makes a speech, wishing each and all a "Happy New Year," in certain cases adding, "and I hope that you, and you," mentioning the names, "will obtain good situations." This is a delicate intimation to the persons named that their services are dispensed with. In ordinary Chinese business affairs all accounts are closed and balanced and all debts paid at the New Year.

In Hong Kong the cessation from business lasts for ten days. At this time booths are erected on either side of several streets in the Chinese quarter, on which are displayed everything that appeals to the fancy of the crowds with which the streets are thronged day and night. There is an enormous sale of a white bell-shaped flower, something like a large erica, known as the New Year flower; goldfish in glass globes are a favourite purchase, and on the stalls rigged up under cover are thousands of articles to suit the fancy of all classes. The heterogeneous stocks-in-trade are evidently got together by roving pedlars or collectors, who find their annual harvest at New Year. Here may be purchased everything, from a piece of bronze or porcelain to a small clay figure, of which a dozen may be bought for a couple of cents. Sometimes an article of real value may be picked up by a seeker after second-hand chances, while eager children spend their cents in smaller investments; but the annual bazaar has one peculiarity that speaks well for the masses of the Chinese people. In all the thousands of articles and pictures exhibited for sale there is not to be seen the slightest indication of even a suspicion of immodesty.

Over every door is now found a small ornament of peacock's feathers, that being a lucky emblem. The social ceremonies are many and elaborate. New Year visits of congratulation are paid; the family graves are visited, and due honours paid to the dead; and presents are offered and accepted. During the holidays immense quantities of fire-crackers are exploded, a string costing many dollars being sometimes hung from an upper balcony, the explosion of the crackers, with loud sounding bombs at intervals, lasting for several minutes, and filling the street with apparently the sharp crackle of musketry and the boom of heavy guns. At the end of the festival the streets are filled with the vermilion paper that covered the exploded fireworks.

Next to the New Year's fair, the most interesting study in Hong Kong was the crowds who came down from Canton and the outlying districts of Kwangtung province for the annual race-meeting— a European institution that flourishes at every coast port in China, the horses being hardy little

Mongolian ponies, and the sport excellent. During the three days' racing it was the custom practically to allow a Saturnalia, and the police closed their eyes to offences against the gambling laws, only pouncing upon faked pu-chee boxes, loaded dice, or other unfair instruments of gambling. On the race-course these gamblers plied their trade between the races, and afforded an opportunity of seeing the most diverse and curious games of chance and skill. One game I do not remember to have seen elsewhere. Round a flat stone was drawn a circle with a diameter of about five feet, divided into spaces radiating from centre to circumference. On the stone the proprietor placed a heap of copper coin. The players placed their stakes in any division chosen; then the proprietor placed a weight on his head, from which he jerked it at a distance of about twelve feet. If the weight hit the heap of coin he took the stakes, but if it fell on one of the divisions, the player who staked on that division took the heap of coin on the stone.

Again, on a board was painted a number of Chinese characters, on any one of which the players placed their stakes. The proprietor then handed a bag to a player, who took out a handful of disks, like draughtsmen, on each of which was a character. The handful was placed on the table and sorted, each character being placed on the corresponding character on the board. The player received as many times his stakes as there were characters drawn corresponding to that on which he had placed his money. If no corresponding character was drawn, then he lost.

In pursuance of a determined effort to stop the ravages of plague, the custom of winking at what were undoubtedly irregularities was abandoned, so as to check the influx of the many thousands of "sporting" vermin to Hong Kong at race time, and once stopped the custom could not be permitted to again establish itself.

It must not be assumed that all the interests of Hong Kong are exhausted by a cursory or even a lengthened examination of its streets and outdoor amusements. Hong Kong boasts of excellent schools, the Queen's College and St. Joseph's Schools being the largest. There is an excellent boarding-school for the sons and daughters of Chinese gentlemen, where the utmost care is exercised in the supervision of the pupils ; a medical college exists in which the entire course of medical education can be taken ; and it is now proposed to establish a university that may yet be the centre of higher education for Chinese students.

The charities of China are not sufficiently realized ; but while there is no general organization of charitable societies, as in European countries, individual charity is widespread. The poor receive gifts of clothing in winter ; in times of famine or of scarcity rice is often distributed free, or sold under cost price, or coffins are supplied to the poor. In Hong Kong the Chinese community have built a well equipped hospital for general patients, and also a plague hospital for the reception of the victims of this scourge that has annually visited the city for the past fifteen years.

There is also in connection with the " Tung Wa " hospital an institution called the Pow-li-un-kok, where orphan children are taken, as are also received the children who from time to time are rescued by the police from harpies who are carrying them through Hong Kong for the purpose of selling them as domestic slaves. These children are brought up, and the boys placed in situations where they can earn their living, while arrangements are made for the marriage of the girls when they reach a marriageable age. Chinese frequently take girls from the institution as wives. It is also used as a rescue home for fallen and friendless girls for whom also husbands are often found.

These are but brief sketches of phases of Chinese life as it presents itself to one who has had no opportunity for the study of cause and effect that would require long years of careful observation. We know but little of the real China. The average European, if he thinks of China at all, sets her down as a nation just emerging from barbarism, untruthful, deceitful, and having more than her share of original sin. On the other hand, the Chinese who have come in contact with foreign Powers regard them as bullies, who have by their destructive prowess forced themselves upon the Middle Kingdom and deprived the Emperor and his government of their sovereignty over the various concessions at the treaty ports. No definite complaint has been formulated on this matter so far; but it must not be assumed that there is no feeling of irritation on the subject in the minds of many of the educated Chinese. The phenomenal successes of Japan in war, and the rapidity with which she has compelled her acceptance on terms of equality by foreign nations, has set the Chinese a-thinking, and we know not how soon the demand for reconsideration of foreign relations may become inconveniently pressing.

The death of the late Dowager-Empress and of the young Emperor, whose sudden and mysterious death was the crowning tragedy of years of sorrow and restraint, has placed upon the Imperial throne an infant whose father (the Regent) is a prince of enlightened and progressive views. Already great changes have been made, and greater still are projected. The isolation of centuries is being modified, and in nearly three thousand schools in

135

CHINA

China the English language is being taught, and
Western methods of instruction are being
introduced. Many internal reforms are being
considered, and the principle of the training
to arms of all young men has been decided
upon. If we take even one-tenth of the
population as being liable to military training, it
would give a crop of recruits of forty millions ! It
remains to be seen if such an evidence of power
will set in motion the military instinct, or if a
different system of education may not result in a
demand for drastic changes in the whole system
and constitution of government. There is in the
Southern Provinces a strong leaven of opinion
formed by students who have been trained in
the colleges of the United States. Their aspirations
are mainly on Republican lines ; but I do not find
that this solution commends itself to the people
of the Northern Provinces.

The establishment of local councils has been
decided upon, the inevitable result of which will
be the lessening of the autocratic power of provincial
officials. Whether the change will result in the
increase of efficiency or the decrease of corruption
time alone will tell ; but we may rest assured that
however loudly reformers may demand changes of
system and custom, the present generation will be
very slow to move. When the Chinese people do

move the advance will be probably steady, and will certainly be maintained. Should a military instinct be evolved, an alliance with Japan might at a future period form the strongest combination in the world, and when that time arrives the present system of extra-territoriality of the concessions, so convenient for foreigners, will go by the board.

At present, however, China offers in her markets an object for the keen competition of the manufacturing nations of the world, in which the British manufacturer bids fair to be beaten, especially by our friends in Germany, whose watchword in commerce, as in everything besides, is " thorough."

The awakening of China means her entrance into strong competition for her full share of the trade of the world. With her great commercial capacity and enormous productive power she will be able to a large extent to supply her own wants, and will certainly reach out to distant foreign markets. Exploration discloses the fact that in bygone ages Chinese influence has reached to the uttermost parts of the globe. It is to be found in the ornaments of the now extinct Bæthucs of Newfoundland, and in the buried pottery of the Incas of Peru, while in Ireland a number of Chinese porcelain seals have been discovered at different times and in some cases at great depths, the period, judging from the characters engraved upon them, being about the ninth century A.D. It may be that with the increase of commercial activity, wages will rise to such an extent as to bring the cost of production in China to the level of that of other nations; if not, then the future competition may produce results for the wage-earners of Liverpool, Birmingham, and Manchester evoking bitter regret that the policy of coaxing, worrying, bullying, and battering the Far Eastern giant into the path of commercial energy has been so successful. Given machinery, cheap labour, unsurpassed mineral deposits, and educated determination to use them, and China will prove a competitor before whom all but the strongest may quail.

The only competition for which she will never enter is a competition in idleness. Every man works to the full extent of his capacity, and the virile vigour of the nation is intact.

With the coming change in her educational system that will strike off the fetters of competitive memorizing and substitute rational reflection, China must be a potent factor in the affairs of the world. When that time comes let us hope that the relations between China and the British Empire will be the outcome of mutual confidence and goodwill.